T0346696

BETTER
BRAND
HEALTH

OXFORD

UNIVERSITY PRESS

BETTER
BRAND
HEALTH

**Measures and Metrics for
a *How Brands Grow* World**

JENNI ROMANIUK

OXFORD
UNIVERSITY PRESS

Oxford University Press is a department of the University of Oxford.
It furthers the University's objective of excellence in research,
scholarship, and education by publishing worldwide. Oxford is a registered
trademark of Oxford University Press in the UK and in certain other countries.

Published in Australia by
Oxford University Press
Level 8, 737 Bourke Street, Docklands, Victoria 3008, Australia.

 A catalogue record for this
book is available from the
National Library of Australia

ISBN 9780190340902

Reproduction and communication for educational purposes
The Australian *Copyright Act 1968* (the Act) allows educational institutions that
are covered by remuneration arrangements with Copyright Agency to reproduce
and communicate certain material for educational purposes. For more
information, see copyright.com.au.

Edited by Karen Jayne
Typeset by Newgen KnowledgeWorks Pvt. Ltd., Chennai, India
Proofread by Pete Cruttenden
Printed in China by Leo Paper Products Ltd.

Disclaimer
Aboriginal and Torres Strait Islander peoples are advised that this publication may include images or
names of people now deceased.

Links to third party websites are provided by Oxford in good faith and for information only. Oxford
disclaims any responsibility for the materials contained in any third party website referenced in this work.

CONTENTS

THE CASE FOR BRAND HEALTH TRACKING

Brand health tracking is expensive, time consuming and results in large PowerPoint decks that provide little insight—so why do it at all? Can't we just get all this information from the wealth of data easily available online? Why bother with the time and cost of interviewing online panellists?

These are sensible questions to ask. Building profitable brands is a challenging endeavour. We pit our best efforts against those of competitors, to a sea of largely inattentive category buyers. While ultimately the success of our endeavours is revealed in buying behaviour, the initial battle is fought in the minds of category buyers. We can't see this battle—it typically happens in the memory, in the moment. But with the right metrics, we can check if we have laid sufficient groundwork to give a brand the best chance of success when that moment presents itself. This is the valuable role that research can play—*to provide a window into the mind of the category buyer.*

The most common instrument marketers use to investigate category buyer memories is the 'brand health tracker'. This is a survey of category buyers designed to capture their thoughts and feelings about brands in the category. These surveys can be up to 30 minutes long, and the data collected becomes those lengthy PowerPoint reports. Despite the length, or perhaps because of it, marketers commonly complain about the challenges of extracting value from these reports. It's like you pay a research agency to build a haystack and (hopefully) hide a couple of needles of insight inside for you to find.

A worthy objective of brand health research is to document a brand's readiness to compete mentally, by taking stock of the memories category buyers hold for the category and its brands. This *could* be one of the most useful pieces of information a company gets about the efficacy of past marketing activities, the brand's likely future trajectory and competitor threats. Unfortunately, current brand health tracking efforts often fall short due to philosophy, fads and fear:

- *Philosophy* – Most trackers were developed in a time when it was common to prioritise the heavy/loyal buyer. This leads to misguided measures and metrics.

- *Fads* – New measures are often added so everyone feels the tracker is up to date with current trends, irrespective of their value. This leads to bloated questionnaires.

- *Fear* – A fear of losing 'tracking' ability means rarely are measures dropped, even when they wane in popularity. These results just get moved further back into the slide deck, until they get sent to the 'kiss of death' section—the appendix. This leads to bloated reports.

Therefore, despite the promise of providing insight into the brand's place in the category buyer's mind, prognosticating via brand health tracking is less evidence-based and often more like divination via reading chicken entrails.

This book is about improving the quality of brand health tracking. It addresses three of the most common problems that plague current tracking instruments:

1 *Measuring the wrong things* – Many survey instruments are not built for a Laws of Growth world, and so emphasise concepts that don't add value or insight into brand growth and neglect ones that do.

2 *Measuring the right things in the wrong way* – Sometimes the *what* is correct, but the *how* is faulty, which then compromises the quality of the output.

3 *Poor interpretation* – The devil is not in the detail but in the context. Many metrics lack any context other than what was achieved last wave, which makes misinterpretation more likely.

The aim of this book is to go back to basics and provide you with the knowledge and tools to shift to a more effective, efficient, concise and evidence-based category buyer memory tracker. For those setting up new trackers, the book contains advice on question wording, questionnaire structure and analysis approaches. Additional resources such as questionnaire templates are available at www.jenniromaniuk.com to help you in this process. For those with existing trackers, I hope this book helps you improve the quality of your current research and provides ideas for future improvements.

Lack of movement in metrics is another common complaint from marketers and sometimes that is a problem of our own making. Therefore, where possible, the book also covers what is normal for metrics, what changes to expect, and where to look when you expect to see changes in metrics, but nothing happens. While this isn't a book on marketing activity effectiveness, it does touch on the topic as the effects of marketing activity should be apparent in brand health metrics. When it is not, it could be the measurement approach, but it could also reflect a failing in the marketing activity. Again, where possible, the book contains common shortcomings in the execution of marketing activities that could be holding back your brand.

Given the ubiquity of online data, companies are looking to alternatives such as passive monitoring of online conversations to understand category buyers' thoughts and feelings about brands. Therefore, we also explore the value of non-survey-based approaches and highlight the opportunities and limitations of this data.

This book is written for:
- *marketing/brand managers* who rely on brand health metrics to assess performance and highlight future opportunities/threats
- *insights managers* who commission this type of research, and want to improve their research briefs, ability to evaluate provider suggestions, as well as questionnaire design, analysis and reporting skills
- *market researchers* who design questionnaires, collect data and create reports, and who want to improve the quality, relevance and cost effectiveness of the work they do
- *marketing educators* who want to teach evidence-based market brand health research practices
- *marketing students* who want to learn best practice from the outset.

In some sections it does get into the weeds and deals with the specifics of measurement such as wording and scale construction. You can skip those geeky bits if you just want a higher-level understanding and are not actually designing questionnaires yourself. It's also not a modelling book as there are no complicated statistical analyses; it's all able to be done with basic analysis programs.

I do want to apologise to my past clients! I have not always employed all the recommendations in this book. When creating this book, re-reading past research, conducting additional research, and putting all this information together forced me to realise where some of my own practices can be improved. I also learnt a great deal while writing this book. I promise to enact these ideas more comprehensively in the future.

This book is also self-serving, as poor surveys provide poor data and this is a lost R&D opportunity. The more people that collect good quality data, the more we can learn. If you adopt this approach and want to give data back to the academic research community, then please email me. Your 'old' data can have a second life and be useful for our future R&D.

Happy tracking!

Jenni

ABOUT THE AUTHOR

Dr Jenni Romaniuk is Research Professor and Associate Director (International) of the Ehrenberg–Bass Institute at the University of South Australia. Jenni's research focuses on building and measuring brand memories. This covers brand equity, mental availability, brand health metrics, distinctive assets and word of mouth. She is also a pioneer in measures and metrics for Distinctive Assets, Category Entry Points and Mental Availability.

She is the lead author of *How Brands Grow Part 2* with Byron Sharp and has also published *Building Distinctive Brand Assets*, both with Oxford University Press.

Jenni is a past executive editor of the *Journal of Advertising Research*, and she now sits on the journal's Senior Advisory Board and is Associate Editor of the *International Journal of Market Research*. Jenni was awarded the University of South Australia Business School's Distinguished Researcher in 2020.

www.JenniRomaniuk.com

CONTRIBUTORS

Magda Nenycz-Thiel is a Research Professor at the Ehrenberg–Bass Institute. Magda's main areas of research are category growth, physical availability, private labels, portfolio management, e-commerce and innovation. As the founder and leader of the Industry Growth Initiative, Magda has developed a team of researchers focused on category growth research, and they apply their discoveries to improve how companies make growth investments. Currently, Magda's focus is helping organisations to transform into an evidence-based culture to grow categories and brands more successfully. She has published widely in academic journals including *Journal of Advertising Research*, *Marketing Letters* and the *European Journal of Marketing*.

Anne Sharp is a Professor of Marketing, Senior Marketing Scientist and founding member of the Ehrenberg–Bass Institute. Much of Anne's work has the common theme of applying marketing science knowledge to sustainable marketing. She helps organisations understand human behaviour around sustainability so they can develop and market better products, ideas, campaigns and engagement strategies. Anne also has a focus on ethics and research integrity. She has been a full member of the Market Research Society for over 20 years, teaches market research at both the undergraduate and postgraduate level, and serves as a University of South Australia ethics chair and advisor. Anne has published over 50 academic papers, with her work appearing in respected journals such as the *European Journal of Marketing* and the *International Journal of Research in Marketing*. In her research Anne forges partnerships with governments, regulatory bodies and commercial entities.

ACKNOWLEDGMENTS

The author and the publisher wish to thank the following copyright holders for reproduction of their material.

Chap. 7: Extract on p. 108 reproduced with permissions from Romaniuk, J. and B. Sharp (2000). Using known patterns in image data to determine brand positioning. *International Journal of Market Research*, **42**(2): 219–230. https://doi.org/10.1177/147078530004200205. **Chap. 8:** Extract on p. 123 reproduced with permissions from Batra, R., A. Ahuvia and R. Bagozzi (2012). Brand Love. *Journal of Marketing*, **76**(2): 1–16. https://doi.org/10.1509/jm.09.0339. **Chap. 9:** Extract on p. 144 used with permission from Banelis, M., E. Riebe and C. Rungie (2013). Empirical evidence of repertoire size. *Australasian Marketing Journal*, **21**(1): 59–65; Extract on p. 147 used with permission from Ludwichowska, G., J. Romaniuk and M. Nenycz-Thiel (2017). Systematic response errors in self-reported category buying frequencies. *European Journal of Marketing*, **51**(7/8): 1440–1459; Extract on p. 152 used with permission from Banelis, M., E. Riebe and C. Rungie (2013). Empirical evidence of repertoire size. *Australasian Marketing Journal*, **21**(1): 59–65. **Chap. 10:** Extract on p. 165 from Kalwani, M. U. and A. J. Silk (1982). On the Reliability and Predictive Validity of Purchase Intention Measures. *Marketing Science*, **1**(3): 243–286; Morwitz, V. G., J. H. Steckel and A. Gupta (2007). When do purchase intentions predict sales? *International Journal of Forecasting*, 23(3): 347–364; Wright, M. and M. MacRae (2007). Bias and variability in purchase intention scales. *Journal of the Academy of Marketing Science*, **35**(4): 617–624; **Chap. 13:** Extract on p. 196 used with permission from Amazon Preview, Frequently Asked Questions.

1

Applying the Laws of Growth to Brand Health Tracking

JENNI ROMANIUK

A useful brand health tracker has a foot in the past and an eye on the future. It provides the information for marketers to diagnose the impact of that past marketing activity on category buyers and use these results to prescribe actions to improve the brand's future performance.

By looking at the category through a Laws of Growth lens we can identify the desirable changes in category buyer memories. This helps us improve brand health research at all stages, from sample selection to how we interpret the results.

This chapter briefly recaps three of the most important empirical Laws of Brand Growth[1] and applies the learnings from these laws to brand health tracking. These three laws explain how brands grow and compete, and together they highlight the brand and buyer priorities to monitor.

---

1   For more detail read *How Brands Grow Parts 1 & 2*.

The outcome of this integration of marketing science into brand health tracking is summarised in the following mantra:

Design for the category, analyse for the buyer, report for the brand.

The brand is important, but first designing the research via the category lens creates a more robust view for now as well as into the future. Second, incorporating the key influence of past buying on the category buyer that holds these memories improves our data analysis. Finally, interpreting the results within the context of brand size improves our ability to extract insights from the data. To signal this change in tracker philosophy, we call the approach encapsulated by this book a category buyer memory (CBM) tracker.

We will now recap the key laws of growth to understand their influence on the foundations of a CBM tracker.

Empirical law 1: Brands grow mainly by penetration, adding buyers to their customer base in each time period

For many decades marketers have treated the answer to the question of how brands grow as either an unknown, dependent on context, or a strategic choice they get to make. However, the empirical evidence says there is a consistent answer—that brands grow by getting more category buyers to buy their brand in any time period (a.k.a brand penetration strategy). This finding generalises across a wide range of categories, countries and buyer types, and has persisted over time (e.g., Stern and Ehrenberg 2002; McDonald and Ehrenberg 2003; Romaniuk et al. 2014; Nenycz-Thiel et al. 2018).

When brands grow, brand loyalty also rises, but usually only when accompanied by a much larger change in penetration (e.g., three times). This loyalty lift is most likely a by-product of a successful penetration growth strategy because activities that impact the brand's non-buyers also tend to reach the brand's current buyers. Think of it as a brand growth 'rising tide' that lifts all boats (segments), but that it is only via reaching very light/non-buyers can sufficient groundswell be created to get a sustainable lift.

This pattern is expressed in the Double Jeopardy (DJ) law (e.g., Ehrenberg et al. 1990), which says that small brands suffer twice, as they have fewer buyers who are slightly less loyal, when compared to bigger brands. Brand loyalty (how much/often customers buy) and penetration (how many category buyers buy) both follow a predictable pattern because they are determined by the brand's market share. Therefore, two brands with the same market share will usually have very similar brand buying metrics—you can't choose your brand's loyalty score now, or if it changes share.

DJ law also holds across different loyalty measures. For example, in service categories, number of product holdings and retention rate are common loyalty metrics, while in packaged goods, the 'go to' loyalty metrics are purchase frequency/buy rate and share of category requirements. These different metrics all display DJ patterns. Metrics from different buyer types (e.g., B2B, subscription) and from buyers in different countries, such as the United States, China, Kenya, Brazil and the Kingdom of Saudi Arabia, also show the DJ pattern.

Table 1.1 shows DJ in visitation of social media sites, where brands vary more in percentage of weekly visitors (penetration) than frequency of weekly visitation (loyalty). A smaller site such as Vevo suffers twice as it has fewer visitors, who visit its site slightly less often than visitors of bigger social media sites, such as Instagram or YouTube.

Table 1.1: Social media/messaging site visitation, United States

	Share of visits (%)	Weekly penetration (%)	Average number of visits per week
Facebook	20.8	69	8.2
YouTube	18.6	64	7.9
Instagram	12.5	45	7.5
Facebook Messenger	11.1	46	6.6
TikTok	8.9	28	8.5
Snapchat	7.8	26	8.1
Twitter	6.4	25	7.1
Pinterest	4.0	18	6.1
WhatsApp	3.1	11	7.7
Reddit	2.9	12	6.5
LinkedIn	2.0	10	5.6
Tumblr	0.8	3	7.0
WeChat	0.5	2	6.7
Vevo	0.4	2	6.1
Average	**7.1**	**26**	**7.1**

Data from Ehrenberg-Bass Institute survey, n=820

The DJ law shows us what metrics should look like for a brand of a specific share, but there can be exceptions. This is the second value of the DJ law, which is to reveal when metrics are unusually high or low for a brand, given its size. For example (see Table 1.1), WhatsApp and Reddit have a similar share of occasions; however, WhatsApp has lower penetration and higher frequency from its visitors compared to Reddit. In the context of WhatsApp's size and the DJ law, we can see that WhatsApp visitation metrics are unusual and therefore worth investigating further. Deviations from the DJ law usually reveal a weakness in the brand that needs to be addressed before the brand can fully realise its growth potential.

The DJ law also lets us plot what will happen when a brand grows in share. For example, for Pinterest to reach the visitor metrics of Instagram, it needs to acquire 2.5 times more visitors (18% to 45%) who will visit the site 1.4 times more (6.1 to 7.5 usage occasions per week). The 'non/light-buyer' brains who will be responsible for this extra penetration are an important audience for a CBM tracker to measure.

The DJ law also shows us what brand decline will look like. If Twitter declines to Reddit's level, it will lose over half its visitors (from 25% to 12%) and those remaining will use Twitter around 10% less often (7.1 to 6.5 times a week). The change in brand performance manifests as *much* lower penetration and *slightly* lower loyalty.

The memories of the brand's non/light-buyers also play a role in a brand's sales decline. All brands lose customers, even growing brands; however, there is evidence that brand decline comes from failure to acquire sufficient non-buyers to replace buyer loss (e.g., Riebe et al. 2014). Therefore, insight into the memories of a brand's non-buyers could be an early-warning system that growth efforts are ineffective for this segment.

Implications of the DJ law for CBM tracking

Brands could grow via different penetration versus loyalty paths, due to a unique mix of strategies, tactics and circumstances. But they don't. The persistent and consistent path to brand growth means we all have the same objective, and are playing on the same field with the same rules. Therefore, the greatest advantage you can have is if you learn to play the game well.

This means allowing the responses from all category buyers to be heard, particularly ones that are important for growth but are harder to hear.

Brands grow through getting more category buyers to be brand buyers in any time period. This means the leading indicators for growth are likely to lie within the memories of any brand's very light/non-buyers. Two important characteristics of your brand's very light/non-buyers are:

1 when compared to brand buyers they give much lower scores for the brand on all brand health metrics

2 they often buy other brands and so are more predisposed to respond about these competitors instead of your brand, meaning any responses about your brand from this segment are often going to be buried under responses for other brands.

Therefore, measures that capture responses that are (relatively) low, and often latent, will more effectively track brand non-buyer category buyer memory.

The 'penetration versus loyalty' debate

The implications of the Laws of Growth are often reduced to a 'penetration versus loyalty' debate, where two paths enter the arena but only one will triumph. This is a false dichotomy. In the early days, Andrew Ehrenberg converted this into a 'penetration-rules' message as a provocative way to counter the 'loyalty loyalists' at the time. It has never been either/or but both, but not equally. Brands grow by having (many) more buyers who buy the brand (a little) more (as outlined in *How Brands Grow*, Sharp 2010).

A simple 'penetration-rules' message works in practice because marketing activities that are able to affect very light/non-buyers usually also impact current buyers of the brand. Brand buyers are more likely to notice advertising for brands they use than brands they don't (e.g., Vaughan et al. 2016). Therefore, reaching the 'hard to reach' gets you those buyers and everyone else too. 'Loyalty loyalists' are yet to provide convincing evidence that tactics aimed at building loyalty will also result in acquisition/penetration growth.

The clear story about how brands grow does not mean it is easy to grow brands. It just means we know what success looks like. It is up to us how quickly we travel down that path, or if we take time and resource-consuming detours.

Does that mean we ignore current brand buyers?

When a brand grows, loyalty also grows, just at a much lower rate than penetration. This means that understanding the impact of marketing activity on current buyers is also important, because marketing activity has a role in staving off a sales decline (more on this in Chapter 11). A buyer can decrease their brand purchases if there is:

- *preference change – I previously liked it, now I don't.*
  A decline in preference is a conscious process and so is easier to pick up via direct questioning (more on this in Chapter 8 on Brand Attitude).
- *memory erosion – I forgot about it.*
  Memory erosion is a gradual process that happens when memory is not refreshed. This makes it harder to notice or survey, as we rarely remember what we have forgotten (more on this in Chapter 5 on Mental Availability).

Empirical law 2: Brand buyer profiles hardly differ across competitive brands

Is your brand's target buyer female household shoppers aged 25–45 years? Or Millennials or Gen Z? Or women aged 35–55 years who care about the environment and donate to animal welfare charities? In a world of scarce resources, it is often assumed the sensible decision is to narrow your marketing efforts to an optimal segment of the market. However, the evidence suggests otherwise. Your brand's buyer profile should follow the category buyer profile.

Studies that compare brand buyer profiles in competitive markets find it is normal for competing brand buyer profiles to be very similar (e.g., Uncles et al. 2012; Anesbury et al. 2017; Patrick et al. 2018).

Table 1.2 illustrates the law with an example from the fast food category in Turkey. While the brands are functionally different from each other, the buyer profiles are very similar. All brands have similar proportions of buyers in the older and younger category, buyers from larger or smaller households, buyers having kids of different ages or no kids, and buyers who are working and with different income levels. This lack of variation in the profile of competing brands is normal.

If your brand's profile differs from the category profile, this usually reveals an impediment to growth so you should be scrutinising rather than celebrating customer base skews. For example, Sultanahmet Köftecisi should not be celebrating it has more customers aged between 25 and 34 years but wondering why it has fewer customers aged between 18 and 24 years than other brands.

Table 1.2: Brand user profile examples across fast food, Turkey

| | Male % | Age % | | | | No. people in household % | | |
		18–24 years	25–34 years	35–49 years	50–65 years	One person	3 to 5 people	6+ people
Total	67	27	41	28	3	5	75	4
Burger King	67	28	41	28	3	5	74	4
Domino's	70	26	44	27	3	5	77	3
KFC	68	28	46	24	3	5	74	5
Little Caesars	66	30	41	23	6	5	71	3
McDonald's	68	25	42	30	3	5	78	2
Popeyes	64	30	35	33	2	3	80	5
Sbarro	68	32	33	32	2	5	74	3
Sultanahmet Köftecisi	63	18	47	29	6	4	75	7

| | Kids at home % | | | Full-time work % | Income % | | | |
	<2 years	10–16 years	No children		Under 1500 TL	1500 to 2000 TL	2000 to 3000 TL	3000 TL or more
Total	11	13	40	64	17	11	21	46
Burger King	10	14	43	62	17	12	24	42
Domino's	11	13	38	63	21	10	23	42
KFC	12	12	45	64	17	12	19	46
Little Caesars	11	13	50	58	17	8	20	50
McDonald's	11	16	37	64	19	12	23	43
Popeyes	12	13	36	67	16	6	22	51
Sbarro	10	13	40	65	16	13	17	52
Sultanahmet Köftecisi	14	12	34	68	13	13	23	46

Data collected by the Ehrenberg-Bass Institute, n=800

Brand growth comes less from finding an optimal target market, and is more about the brand's feasible market—the buyers it could have (Graham and Kennedy 2021). The brand's feasible buyer profile should mirror the category's buyer profile, unless there are some category buyers who cannot buy from you (i.e., you do not offer a gluten-free option, so gluten-intolerant category buyers are outside of your feasible category buyer base).

Implications of brand user profiles hardly differ law for CBM tracking

Do not let any brand-specific target market assumptions contaminate your sample recruitment plan. The sample profile should follow a normal category buyer profile to get a realistic picture of the brand's current situation and future opportunities/challenges.

You can always isolate a specific segment in the analysis stage, but it is hard to get good quality insights if you bias your sample recruitment from the outset.

Empirical law 3: Your brand's main competitors are (almost always) the biggest brands in the category

When it comes to competition, it's a cliché, but size matters! The Duplication of Purchase (DoP) law states that brands typically compete with other brands in line with the competitor brand's popularity. Table 1.3 shows examples of the data from social media sites in the United States, where around 80% of every social media site users also visited Facebook in the last week, while only around 40% had also visited Twitter.[2]

The DoP law first emerged from Goodhardt and Ehrenberg's (1969) analysis of TV viewing data. Since then, researchers have found it present in a wide range of categories, including unusual categories such as long-haul travel, luxury brand buying, hospitality and gaming (Dawes et al. 2009; Lam and Ozorio 2013; Lynn 2013; Romaniuk and Sharp 2016).

---

2 We can also see the Natural Monopoly law (Dawes 2020), whereby the biggest brand(s) monopolise light category users, and so share less with every other brand. Facebook, and to a lesser extent YouTube, shares fewer customers with other social media sites (row average of 45–50% compared to around 65% for other sites).

Table 1.3: One week duplication of visitation for social media sites in the United States (sample of brands)

	Pen %	Facebook	YouTube	Instagram	TikTok	Twitter	Pinterest
Facebook	76		75	53	34	34	30
YouTube	72	79		59	40	40	35
Instagram	52	77	82		50	48	38
TikTok	34	76	85	76		47	44
Twitter	33	79	88	76	49		40
Pinterest	30	77	84	67	52	45	
Average	**49**	**78**	**83**	**66**	**45**	**43**	**37**

If a brand grows, it will gain more additional buyers from bigger competitors, and fewer from smaller competitors. If a brand declines, that brand will lose more additional buyers to those same bigger competitors, and fewer to the smaller competitors (e.g., Romaniuk 2021b).

There are deviations from this pattern, such as excess sharing between two or more brands, often based on functional similarities. Functional lookalikes can still be useful to monitor, but typically are not as important to your brand's future trajectory as the bigger brands in the category.

Implications of the DoP law for CBM tracking

The DoP law helps us understand the relationships between competitive brands from a category buyer and brand growth/decline perspective. This knowledge helps us prioritise competitors for:
- *opportunities* – where customers will come from if your brand grows
- *threats* – where customers will go if your brand declines.

This law tells us that the competitor lists in our tracking research need to be comprehensive, include all bigger and medium share brands, and include all, or a representative set, of smaller share brands. Don't bias the brand list to just include your own brand's lookalikes in function, positioning or targeting efforts. Your brand list should be sufficiently comprehensive that it could be used by any brand in the category.

Underlying philosophy for brand health tracking

These three Laws of Growth have important implications for brand health tracking. These laws culminate in a simple underlying philosophy aimed at maximising the knowledge gained from CBM research efforts:

Design for the category, analyse for the buyer, report for the brand.

A CBM instrument that works is one that considers the Laws of Growth in design, analysis and interpretation. This leads to these three underlying principles:

1 *Design for the category* – Your CBM measurement instrument should be one that any brand in the category could use. In the next chapters, we will talk about what this means for areas such as screening for sample inclusion or creating brand lists.

2 *Analyse for the buyer* – The difference between buyers, most relevant to growth and CBM tracking, is not their gender, age or attitude to life but rather their experience with the brand. In the next chapters, you will see how this affects measures and metrics, and how to use this to your advantage.

3 *Report for the brand* – The biggest difference between brand CBM scores is how many buyers a brand has (penetration/market share). Therefore, you need to adjust metric expectations for a brand's size. In the next chapters, you will see how to make this adjustment and why the effort pays off in improved insights and interpretation.

Chapter summary

This chapter covered three key Laws of Growth and the implications for brand health tracker design:

1 *Double Jeopardy* – Growth comes mainly through expanding the customer base in any time period, which means that understanding how your brand is present in the memories of very light/non-buyers of your brand is key to growth.

2 *Brand user profiles hardly differ* – A brand's customer base profile should mimic that of the category, meaning the tracker sample should be based on category profile.

3 *Duplication of Purchase* – Brands compete with other brands in line with competitor share, meaning that competitors who are tracked should be representative of the category.

These laws mean the underlying principles to remember when putting together your CBM tracker are to: a) design for the category, b) analyse for the buyer and c) report for the brand.

In the next chapter we consider one of the most common brand health metrics tracked: Brand Awareness.

2

Brand Awareness

JENNI ROMANIUK

The enduring appeal of Brand Awareness is rooted in its apparent simplicity. That a buyer first needs to be aware of a brand to have any hope of buying is both logical and easy to understand. However, what seems simple on the surface gets complicated quite quickly when you consider Brand Awareness is underpinned by two measurement approaches and three metrics.

This chapter unpacks the relationship between the idea of Brand Awareness, its two most common measurement approaches, and the three most common metrics derived from these measures. It shows how unprompted Brand Awareness measures under-report memories from key brand growth audiences and highlights the challenges when interpreting changes in unprompted Brand Awareness scores over time.

This research reveals the most useful role of Brand Awareness, which is as an indicator of category membership. The best measure to understand the brand's relative performance on this role is prompted awareness of a brand's non-buyers. This turns the illusion of simplicity into something genuinely simple and useful in a Laws of Growth world.

What is 'Brand Awareness'?

Brand Awareness is analogous to that long-time employee who gets everyone's attention but no one dares question, even when they don't make any sense. Brand Awareness is just so logical in that people need to be aware of a brand to buy it, and that more awareness is better than less awareness; that is, it is heresy to challenge the role of Brand Awareness as a key indicator of brand health.

Brand Awareness is also a metric that non-marketers feel they understand, and so it forms a bridge between the marketing department and other company departments, including a company's board (e.g., Ambler 2003). This makes it attractive to report in company-wide dashboards.

Finally, Brand Awareness also typically benefits from a long history, as even when tracking suppliers change, Brand Awareness is the one part of the questionnaire that often stays the same. Longevity gives marketers a sense of familiarity that is naturally appealing.

But what is Brand Awareness?

A bit of history

Brand Awareness emerged in the 1950s as one of the first branding concepts and is the foundation of most buyer behaviour models such as AIDA (Awareness–Interest–Desire–Action) or Ehrenberg's ATR (Awareness–Trial–Repeat). Brand Awareness has enjoyed over 70 years as part of marketing and market research. You would think, after all this time, there would be a body of evidence articulating the value of Brand Awareness metrics and which metric, under which conditions, you should monitor.

Unfortunately, this is not the case.

Brand Awareness learnings have stagnated because very few academic studies include Brand Awareness measures. Often brand research papers sidestep this issue by asking respondents to select brands they were aware of for studies. Even those that claim to include Brand Awareness rarely include different Brand Awareness measures to compare the relative performance/contribution of each. This has limited academia's opportunity to develop more knowledge about Brand Awareness.

Timing is also relevant to our understanding of Brand Awareness. Brand Awareness came into the marketing lexicon between the 1950s and the 1960s, before knowledge around how humans encode, store and access information in memory was integrated into marketing thinking. This (later) knowledge on how memory works reveals the limitations of Brand Awareness as we know it. Before we go into these limitations, let us first revisit the most common ways to measure Brand Awareness and the metrics that are derived from the data.

Common Brand Awareness measures

In commercial brand health tracking, Brand Awareness measures typically involve a category cue (e.g., *carbonated drinks* or *car insurance*) and two different response types:

1 *Unprompted* – Respondents must recall brands from memory without brand names/images.
2 *Prompted* – When brand names or images are provided, respondents just indicate prior recognition of the brand as a member of the category.

These two measurement approaches create the three most reported metrics:

1 *Top-of-Mind awareness (TOM)* – When the brand is the first recalled unprompted, with the category cue.
2 *Spontaneous awareness* – When the brand is recalled unprompted at all with the category cue (also called total unprompted or unaided awareness).
3 *Prompted awareness* – When the brand is recognised after prompting with both the name/image and the category cue.

One, two or three ways to measure Brand Awareness

Before we dive too deeply into the different metrics, it is important to appreciate that these metrics all draw from the same brand memories. The story we see with each metric varies because some measures are more difficult for category buyers than others. Unprompted retrieval is cognitively more difficult than prompted retrieval; and as for TOM, the brand needs to also be more easily retrieved than every other competitor, which introduces another hurdle (as discussed in Laurent et al. 1995): the more difficult the metric, the less complete the narrative.

While the difference in difficulty affects what is retrieved, research comparing Brand Awareness measures shows that once this difficulty is considered, the three measures provide very similar results (Laurent et al. 1995; Romaniuk et al. 2004). This output similarity reflects the common thread through all Brand Awareness metrics: the category as the retrieval cue. Using the same retrieval cue means accessing the same memory network of associations.

Table 2.1 shows the three metrics side by side for the mobile phone handset category. The Pearson's correlation coefficients are 96% (TOM and spontaneous), 83% (spontaneous and prompted) and 68% (TOM and prompted).[1] Then, Table 2.2 reveals the proportion of responses from non-buyers across four categories. Tables 2.1 and 2.2 show three empirical differences between the Brand Awareness measures:

1   *The absolute score* – The easier the measure, the higher every brand scores, which means prompted Brand Awareness scores are always higher than unprompted scores. For example, the TOM score for Nokia is 3%, but the prompted score for Nokia is 79% (Table 2.1).

2   *The concentration of the metric scores* – The more difficult the measure, the more the responses will be concentrated in a few big brands, while small brands struggle. For example, for TOM, the top two brands account for nearly 90% of all responses, while for prompted awareness those same two top brands account for only 35% of responses (Table 2.1).

---

1   All statistically significant at p<0.05.

3 *Non-buyer responses* – The more difficult the measure, the fewer responses will come from non-brand buyers (Wight 2010). Table 2.2 shows on average 10% of TOM responses are for non-buyers only, while prompted awareness averages around 50% of non-buyer awareness for big brands and 84% for small brands.

Remember that if brands grow, it is non-buyers that will be a key part of that growth. Therefore, a growth-orientated Brand Awareness measure should effectively capture responses from these category buyers. This is where both unprompted approaches fall short compared to prompted Brand Awareness.

Table 2.1: Mobile phone handset Brand Awareness metrics (brands ordered by penetration)

	% Owned in last 2 years	TOM %	Spontaneous %	Prompted %
Samsung Galaxy	48	38	86	92
Apple iPhone	47	44	80	95
Nokia	13	3	32	79
OPPO	8	3	18	52
Huawei	6	2	20	72
HTC	4	<1	7	53
Google Pixel	4	2	20	64
Xiaomi	2	<1	2	26
Aspera	1	0	0	8
Average	15	10	29	60
Top two brands	48	41	83	93
Bottom three brands	2	1	7	33
Average number of brands	1.3	0.9	2.7	5.4

Ehrenberg-Bass Institute Data collected 2020, n=1,225 Australian category buyers

Table 2.2: Percentage of non-buyer responses from each awareness measure (from Wight (2010) plus additional study from 2021)

	All brands				Large brands				Small brands			
	TOM	Spontaneous	Prompted		TOM	Spontaneous	Prompted		TOM	Spontaneous	Prompted	
Whisky	7	40	68		7	33	48		7	45	80	
Shampoo	11	30	56		13	29	48		12	34	78	
Toothpaste	9	39	73		14	35	49		7	41	82	
Mobile phones	20	69	82		14	45	50		14	77	95	
Average	**12**	**45**	**70**		**12**	**36**	**49**		**10**	**49**	**84**	

TOM Brand Awareness is a poor way to capture the responses for small brands and/or to capture the presence of a brand in the memory of non-buyers. In contrast, prompted Brand Awareness gets more responses for small brands and from non-buyers. Spontaneous Brand Awareness sits in the middle—but is that the best of both worlds, or the worst? Every good metric needs an origin story and a mission, so let's go back to the start for Brand Awareness.

Reasons for measuring Brand Awareness

The reason for measuring Brand Awareness usually falls into one of two camps:
1 *Category identification* – To check if the category buyer is aware the brand is a member of a specific category.
2 *Ease to retrieve* – To assess how easily can the category buyer retrieve the brand from memory when given the category cue.

Brand Awareness in a 'category identifier' role

Under this role a Brand Awareness measure aims to detect if the brand is present in the 'right' part of the category buyer memory, as defined by the category cue. For example, 'Do chocolate buyers know *Russell Stover* as a brand of chocolate?' Without awareness as a brand of chocolate, potential buyers might mistake Russell Stover for an insurance firm, a cookware brand, or as someone with whom they went to primary school. None of those other outcomes would help Russell Stover chocolate to be bought.

It is of no great surprise that when faced with a choice between a brand they know and one they do not know, buyers prefer the known brand (Hoyer and Brown 1990; Macdonald and Sharp 2000). Of course, this also means your brand is *at a disadvantage* when a category buyer is unaware of your brand, but aware of others. Therefore, the objective for building Brand Awareness under the category membership role is to *reduce the number of people unaware that the brand is a member of the category.*

Brand buyers, by virtue of their past behaviour, will have close to 100% category membership Brand Awareness. It is the brand's non-buyers that might lack brand-category links. These brand non-buyers can be aware of other brands in the category, and these other brands can inhibit the retrieval of the brand of interest. Retrieval inhibition is more likely with unprompted measures (Anderson and Bower 1979), so a prompted approach is recommended for measuring Brand Awareness in the category identifier role.

Category membership Brand Awareness has particular relevance when brand non-buyers are plentiful. The following include such brands.

- *New brands/line extensions* – New launches face a category full of non-buyers who do not know they exist or what they offer. Measuring Brand Awareness helps you know if marketing efforts have not just drawn attention to the brand, but also put it in the 'right' part of category buyer memory.

- *Small brands* – Small brands have a few buyers, but most category buyers are non-buyers. There could be a substantive non-aware non-buyer segment that needs to learn the brand is a member of the category. Brand Awareness measurement is particularly useful when a small brand suddenly ramps up its marketing activities.

- *Any brand entering a new (sub)category* – When a known brand in one category enters a new category (e.g., from car/home insurance to pet insurance), the brand needs to be also embedded in the second category part of buyer memories. For example, I might know Allianz offers home insurance but not that it offers pet insurance, so unless Allianz gets put in the pet insurance part of my brain, I am unlikely to have it mentally available when I am thinking of pet insurance options. Brand Awareness measurement with the second category cue can detect the effectiveness of the second category link building efforts.

- *Any brand in a category that is growing via penetration* – If a category is growing by penetration, it is attracting an unusually high volume of new category buyers. These new category buyers have low awareness of all brands in the category. Measuring Brand Awareness among this cohort checks the extent to which the brand is known.

- *Any brand in a category with intermittent category buyer membership* – Some categories only have the same category buyers for a period, after which most category buyers leave and are replaced by a new cohort of category buyers (e.g., nappies/diapers whereby people enter the category after childbirth and leave the category as the child is toilet trained). Brand Awareness measurement checks each new cohort knows of the brand.

How to select a category cue

A good Brand Awareness measure needs to describe the category in words that make sense to a category buyer. It also avoids language that may bias what constitutes category membership; for example, using the category of 'banking' may penalise the retrieval of non-bank lenders like building societies or credit unions. Table 2.3 highlights category cue label approaches that hamper quality data collection and more useful alternatives.

Table 2.3: Selecting a category cue

	Avoid	Instead
Breadth	Avoid cue options so narrow they are unrepresentative of the full competitive set (e.g., cola-flavoured drinks)	Develop a cue to cover the wider competitive set
Composition	Avoid combinations of categories so broad that brands are too disparate to be directly linked to the same cue (e.g., toilet, kitchen and bathroom cleaners)	Use a cue with meaning that the buyer is likely to have in memory and produces a realistic competitive set
Wording	Avoid cues too ambiguous or technical and therefore unlikely to be understood by normal people (e.g., fermented drinks)	Use everyday category buyer language

If you are in doubt, test.[2] Compare the results generated from different cues against brand penetration figures. When doing this test, be careful about priming effects, which is where the responses to the first question unduly influence the responses to the next question. A split-sample approach where each person only gets one cue, but different samples of category buyers get different cues, is an effective way to compare cue performance that avoids priming.

Names or images or both

In the brand list, the brand can be provided in word (name) or image (pack or logo) form. Testing shows that images help more when the brand names are similar, but the images are different; for example, brands of pasta often have very similar Italian sounding names, so

---

2   Actually, even if you are confident in your category cue, you still might benefit from testing to check if that confidence is warranted.

adding pack images or logos helps separate these out. Adding images improves accuracy as well as memory, which means Brand Awareness scores can lower as well as rise.

For example, in a test across 15 brands in the banking category, one group was prompted by the brand name only and the other group was given the brand logos, which often, but not always, included brand name text. The overall average was 56% for brand name only and 58% for the logo. For six of the brands there was no difference in results.

However, seven brands had higher scores when the logo was presented.[3] This is consistent with the picture superiority effect, whereby pictures are more easily processed and remembered than words (Paivio and Csapo 1973). However, for another two brands, the logo had lower awareness than the brand name. One brand had recently undertaken a rebranding exercise, so fewer people recognised the new logo compared to the brand name alone, while another brand used a less familiar acronym in the logo not the full name.

Therefore, adding logo or pack images to the brand name benefits brand recognition, particularly for small brands and for logo changes. Remember the goal is not to check if category buyers are aware of the logo, but if category buyers are aware of the brand, so also include the brand name if it is not clearly present in the logo.

Can a drop in prompted awareness be an early warning signal of brand decline?

Prompted awareness is a recognition measure where the category buyer just needs to recognise prior brand exposure in the context of the category. The ease of this task means that if this metric drops then all the brand's memory links have disappeared. By the time you see this in a survey, it is too late. Figure 2.1 shows testing across eight brands that declined in annual market share. There were no substantive changes in the percentage unaware of the brand (6 percentage points (pp) versus 5pp).

---

3   Three are statistically significant at $p<0.05$, two more at $p<0.10$ and two smaller brands trended in this difference but did not pass statistical tests.

Figure 2.1: Changes in % unaware of personal care brands after market share change, China

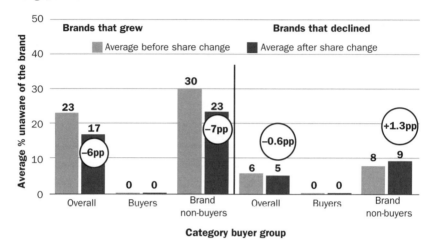

Brand Awareness in an 'ease to retrieve' role

Sometimes Brand Awareness measurement aims to determine how easily category buyers retrieve the brand from memory. Is the brand the first recalled, or the second or the fifth? The underlying premise is that the earlier the brand is recalled, the better chance it has of being bought. While retrievability is important, the 'Brand Awareness' approach to measuring a brand's potential retrievability has two major problems. The first is the unprompted measurement approach, and the second is the use of a single cue retrieval test.

Researchers have likened retrieval from memory to a 'spreading activation'[4] process (in line with, for example, Collins and Loftus 1975). When a retrieval cue is 'activated', the activation spreads down the memory network linked to the cue in category buyer memory. However, as there is a finite amount of effort, not everything linked to the cue is retrieved. The more difficult the retrieval task, the more effort each link

---

4   This idea of 'activation' is a metaphor rather than a reference to an actual concept, but I think it useful to communicate the key ideas rather than go into the complexities of memory. Of the literature on how memory works, I particularly enjoy reading works by Endel Tulving, who has many decades of books and papers to read for those who want more detail.

needs to be retrieved and so the buyer retrieves fewer brands. Therefore, asking category buyers to recall rather than recognise brands reduces the number of brands that reach the memory retrieval threshold. For example, in Table 2.1 prompted measurement generates twice the number of mobile phone brands compared to unprompted measurement (average of 5.4 versus 2.7 brands).

A brand is easier to retrieve from memory when it has received frequent and/or recent reinforcement. This means brands bought in the past will be favoured over brands never bought, and brands with more recent/frequent exposure via buying, using or marketing communications are often favoured over brands where exposure is less recent/frequent. This leads to:

- brand buyers more likely to give a Brand Awareness response than brand non-buyers
- bigger brands (in market share) with more current, recent, heavy and past buyers outperforming smaller brands in Brand Awareness scores.

While prompted Brand Awareness measures also exhibit these qualities, the differences between buyers and brands are exacerbated for unprompted Brand Awareness measures.

With unprompted recall:

- links to the brand give the *possibility* of retrieval, while
- recency and frequency of reinforcement increase the *probability* of retrieval, but
- nothing gives any *certainty* of retrieval.

Someone can fail to retrieve (a.k.a *forget*) a brand they regularly buy, and sometimes a brand that is a vague memory from long ago can just pop into someone's mind. This is what makes human memory both annoying *and* fun.

Retrieval fluctuations become apparent when we examine the same individual's retrieval of brands in response to the same category cue over two separate interviews. Day and Pratt (1971) reported only 54% of the unprompted Brand Awareness responses for household appliance brands were repeated upon re-interview six months later.

Results from more recent data (see Table 2.4) collected three weeks apart from the same category buyers in the soft drinks and financial service categories in the United Kingdom are similar to the research of Day and Pratt (1971). To quantify the stability of Brand Awareness responses, we calculate the repeat rate, which is *the proportion who gave the response in Wave 1 and repeated the response upon re-interview* (taken from Dall'Olmo Riley et al. 1997).

The results across TOM and spontaneous awareness responses show that:

- no brand reaches 100%, with even Coca-Cola only reaching 90% spontaneous Brand Awareness stability; that is, 90% of those who said Coca-Cola unprompted for the first interview repeated Coca-Cola as an unprompted response at the second interview three weeks later
- TOM is less stable than spontaneous Brand Awareness (averages of 28% and 59% compared to 66% and 74%, respectively), which means the more difficult the measure, the less likely the response will be re-retrieved at a later point in time
- smaller brands are often less stable than bigger brands, which is another example of Double Jeopardy (see Chapter 1), as smaller brands not only have initially lower Brand Awareness but also are less likely to be re-retrieved at a later point of time
- responses for soft drink brands are less stable for both metrics than responses for financial services, which suggests the larger the buyers' brand repertoire, the less likely the same brand response will be re-retrieved at a later point in time. This pattern is in line with probabilistic retrieval where the retrieval of any one item is negatively related to how many retrievable alternatives are available.

Therefore, someone retrieving a brand unprompted today does not guarantee they will retrieve that same brand tomorrow, or indeed at any time in the future.

Table 2.4: Individual level awareness response stability over repeat interviews: soft drinks and financial services

Category cue: soft drinks			Category cue: financial services		
	TOM	**Spontaneous**		**TOM**	**Spontaneous**
Coca-Cola	73*	90	Barclays	57	80
Pepsi	40	82	Lloyds	70	78
7UP	11	60	Natwest	53	71
Tango	11	55	HSBC	72	77
Sprite	25	61	Halifax	57	69
Lucozade	10	48	Santander	49	69
Average stability	**28**	**66**	**Average stability**	**59**	**74**

*Interpreted as of those who said Coca-Cola TOM in Wave 1, 73% also said Coca-Cola TOM in Wave 2.

Data collected by the Ehrenberg-Bass Institute, n=954

Past buying and current Brand Awareness

A brand's buyers are more likely to experience conditions that make a brand more retrievable (recency, frequency) than its non-buyers. Further, while a brand's non-buyers can build Brand Awareness via marketing communications, the same brand communications also reaches an even greater proportion of brand buyers. As brand buyers are two to three times more likely to remember exposure to advertising than a brand's non-buyers (e.g., Harrison 2013), an advertisement that reaches 10% of the brand's non-buyers is probably also likely to reach around 20–30% of the brand's buyers.

Therefore, brand buyers have:

• a higher baseline Brand Awareness score due to past brand buying
• a greater propensity to process a brand's advertising.

This means that to detect whether marketing communications successfully built Brand Awareness among a brand's non-buyers, we would need to quarantine brand buyers, so their responses do not drown out non-buyer responses.

TOM and spontaneous Brand Awareness changes over time

When a brand's awareness score changes over time, it is easy to assume all category buyers are equally responsible. However, Wight (2010) examined changes in Brand Awareness over multiple years across three categories and found that the changes were often concentrated in specific buyer groups. For the research, Wight identified when a brand's TOM or spontaneous awareness experienced a statistically significant change between reporting waves. For these instances, he calculated the relative contribution of each buyer group to the difference in the brand's awareness score, and then classified each change into one of three groups:

1 *Buyer dominant* – buyers account for 75% or more of the change.

2 *Shared* – buyers account for between 26% and 74% of the change.

3 *Non-buyer dominant* – buyers account for 25% or less of change.

The results (see Table 2.5) show that changes in TOM awareness are largely concentrated in brand buyers, rather than brand non-buyers needed for growth. Therefore, growth in brand TOM awareness is unlikely to be linked to future growth in sales among very light/non-buyers.

Spontaneous Brand Awareness changes could be buyer dominant (32%), non-buyer dominant (24%) or both (44%). This means you cannot assume that an increase in a brand's overall spontaneous awareness is equal to an increase in non-buyer spontaneous awareness. You need analysis at buyer group level to confirm that non-buyers also grew in spontaneous awareness.

Table 2.5: Buyer sources of changes in TOM and spontaneous awareness scores, results taken from Wight (2010)

	TOM (17 changes)	Spontaneous (74 changes)
Brand buyer dominant	85	32
Shared	15	44
Brand non-buyer dominant	0	24

The category cue as a measure of 'ease to retrieve'

Traditional Brand Awareness retrievability relies on the use of a single category cue as the retrieval test. This is only useful if:

- the category cue is the only cue used to access memory for the purpose of buying, or
- the response to the cue is representative of every other cue that buyers might use to access memory for buying from the category.

Unprompted Brand Awareness measures fail on both criteria. The category cue is not the only cue buyers use to access brands from memory (e.g., Holden 1993, Romaniuk and Sharp 2004), nor is the retrieval from the category cue representative of these other cues that buyers use. If TOM or spontaneous Brand Awareness results are representative of the brand's potential to be retrieved, there should be very few additional responses when testing is expanded beyond the category name to a range of different cues.

We tested this proposition across 12 attributes in the mobile phone handset market (e.g., *Good for someone who likes to keep up with the latest technology* or *protects privacy*). Brand responses for each attribute was also measured via an unprompted approach. The results (see Figure 2.2) show the following Brand Awareness:

- *TOM awareness* – Brands of all sizes gain more responses when the cues are expanded. TOM is a single response, and more cues increase the chance the brand will be that one response for at least one cue. Bigger brands have the greatest absolute percentage point changes, but smaller brands lift tenfold due to the small chance of being TOM with category cue (refer to Table 2.1).
- *Spontaneous awareness* – Again, all brands gain, but this time with similar percentage points across brands of different sizes (6–10 pp).

This means relying on the single category cue will under-represent the retrievability of all brands, but TOM is particularly restrictive for smaller brands.

Figure 2.2: Brand Awareness cue representativeness, Australian mobile phone category

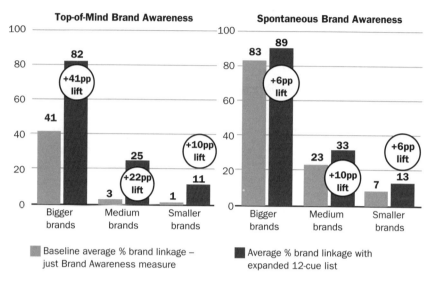

Baseline average % brand linkage – just Brand Awareness measure

Average % brand linkage with expanded 12-cue list

Unprompted Brand Awareness measures also under-report atypical brands

When we use a category label as a cue, the most easily retrievable items tend to be category exemplars, while less typical brands are at a retrieval disadvantage (e.g., Barsalou 1983). For example, Google Pixel[5] is a mobile phone brand, but Google is better known outside the mobile phone market. Across the expanded cue list of 12 attributes, Google gains an average of 17% category buyer responses compared to only 4% for HTC, a brand of similar size in this country/category. Therefore, if Google Pixel relied just on spontaneous awareness as a measure of brand retrieval in the mobile phone category, it would be penalised even more than brands known predominantly as mobile phone brands.

There is no single consideration set

As discussed in *How Brands Grow Part 2* (Romaniuk and Sharp 2021), category buyers do not have a single consideration set that they always use

---

5   To count as aware for Google Pixel, people could state Google, Pixel or both.

when entering the category. Spontaneous Brand Awareness, with a single category cue, cannot replace measurement via a set of context-generated retrieval cues. Each context shapes the retrieval cue buyers will use, and category buyers' memory unconsciously adapts the set of brands to be relevant to that context.

Historically, this was represented as the difference between the 'awareness set' (all known brands) and the 'consideration set' (brands actively considered for buying) (as proposed by Howard and Sheth 1969).[6] This led to a common brand health measure of '*Which brands would you consider for your next purchase?*' This type of question continues with the faulty assumption that there is a singular, stable, context independent set of brands that buyers consider for each purchase. Therefore, tracker questions such as '*Which brands would you consider for purchase?*' do not add value.

The idea of a single consideration set for a category makes little sense if you look at any data or indeed your own behaviour. Last time you wanted *something a bit healthier for dinner*, did you think of the same list of brands as when you last wanted to *treat yourself for dinner*? The last time you wanted to buy a new car for yourself alone to drive, did you have the same brands as if you were buying a new car that you were going to share with your teenage daughter who just got her licence?

Category buyers have many, context-specific, sets of brands that are created ('evoked') each time they buy the category. Chapter 5 on Mental Availability explains a better way of measuring a brand's propensity to be retrieved in buying situations.

Are measurement issues also holding back academic research?

Early academic work in the 1960s tested Brand Awareness in several different ways (e.g., Assael and Day 1968, Axelrod 1968, Gruber 1969). However, these studies rarely controlled for past brand buying (something acknowledged by Axelrod) and could not incorporate later advances in our understanding on how human memory works.

---

6   In case you are curious, the group of brands aware but not considered are referred to as the 'inert set', while the group of brands considered but not bought are referred to as the 'inept' set. I think I would rather be inert than inept!

Over time, the focus of academic research changed, and Brand Awareness became confined to the start of the process; a battle to be fought and won by new brands before moving onto ostensibly more important areas such as brand image, personality or love (Macdonald and Sharp 2003, Hofmann et al. 2021). Therefore, research subjects are often asked to think of their own brands or provided with fictional brands, thus removing any influence of Brand Awareness.

The researchers who include Brand Awareness in their questionnaires often draw on a multi-item scale developed by Yoo and Donthu (2001). This involves rating brands on statements such as '*I can recognise X among competing brands*', '*I am aware of X*' and '*I have no difficulty in imagining [brand X] in my mind*' on a five-point Likert scale (e.g., Dwivedi et al. 2018, Foroudi et al. 2018, Tran et al. 2020). While a scale is attractive if you want to conduct some types of statistical modelling, it is a questionable way to measure that which is, in memory terms, a binary yes/no response. How do you interpret someone's *slightly disagree* response to the statement '*I am aware of brand X*'? This makes these results for this measure of Brand Awareness of questionable usefulness.

A few papers that use industry collected data (rather than their own survey data) purport to include Brand Awareness, but actually use proxy measures. For example, Colicev and colleagues (2018) label the combination of advertising awareness and received WOM as a Brand Awareness measure, while other research focuses on the drivers rather than the consequences of Brand Awareness (Han et al. 2020).

Despite (or perhaps because of) its longevity, Brand Awareness has been largely neglected by academic research. When included in academic research, Brand Awareness is measured poorly or incompletely. This has allowed unprompted Brand Awareness measures to persist in practice with very little scrutiny. Hopefully the research presented encourages you to rethink of the usefulness of Brand Awareness as a measure of retrievability from memory.

How do you change prompted Brand Awareness?

Building prompted Brand Awareness is about ensuring every category buyer knows your brand is a member of X category, whether X is home loans, entertainment or toilet cleaners.

A clearer understanding of the key role of a prompted Brand Awareness measure also clarifies that marketing activity needs these ingredients to lift prompted Brand Awareness:

1 *Reach the brand's non-buyer* – Marketing activity needs to get the attention of brand non-buyers to change their memories.

2 *Include the brand name* – The brand name is the new addition to non-buyer memory, which needs to be a prominent, noticeable part of the marketing activity.

3 *Include category name as an anchor* – The category name puts the brand in the 'right' part of non-buyers' memory. It needs to be near the brand name to form an associative link in non-buyer memory.

Therefore, if building prompted Brand Awareness is an objective of your marketing activities, check all these ingredients are present.

Chapter summary

The most useful role of Brand Awareness measurement is to assess if a category buyer, that is not a brand buyer, recognises the brand as a member of the category. Therefore, the key Brand Awareness metric to monitor is *the percentage of non-buyers aware of the brand*. The objective is to get this as close to 100% as possible.

Non-buyer Brand Awareness is particularly relevant for:

• new launches
• small brands (particularly if they ramp up marketing activities)
• an existing brand entering a new category
• brands in categories expanding in penetration and so have an unusually high influx of new category buyers
• brands in categories where buyers buy from the category for a limited time period.

The category cue should be broad enough to cover the wider range of competitors, avoid biasing to any specific sub-category of brands, and be in a plain language that category buyers both understand and could use to organise their own memory. However, a limitation of prompted Brand Awareness is that it does not easily erode, so it is unhelpful as a sign of brand decline.

What next for unprompted Brand Awareness measures?

All in all, the integration of associative network memory theories into branding research and the empirical results discussed in this chapter call into question the value of unprompted Brand Awareness measures. It appears they are an ineffective short-cut attempt to measure brand retrievability. However, as it is hard to let go of a well-known measure, for those who do want to keep an unprompted Brand Awareness measure in their brand health toolkit, they should:

- choose spontaneous awareness over TOM Brand Awareness, as there is no evidence that TOM is useful as a growth or decline indicator
- separate out the spontaneous awareness metrics for brand buyers and non-buyers to get a more direct measurement of the impact on Brand Awareness building activities on the brand's non-buyers.

That will at least give you more sensitive spontaneous Brand Awareness metrics, and a better ability to judge its usefulness over time.

3

Brand Attributes: Selection

JENNI ROMANIUK

One of the longest sections of any brand tracker questionnaire is the aptly named brand attribute battery. Attributes within a list can range from the common, such as *trustworthy* or *innovative*, to the 'on trend', such as *is a socially responsible brand* or *embraces diversity*, to the kind of weird, such as *a brand I feel close to*, or *hard to resist*. This list is designed to capture how category buyers perceive the brand on qualities that are important for buying, which is then compared to how category buyers perceive competitors on the same qualities.

Brand attribute measurement involves several parts, to be covered over the next few chapters. These parts include decisions on which attributes to track, and how to word these attributes; and how to measure brand performance, and how to analyse the data.

As the sexiest analysis in the world will not compensate for poor attribute selection, the first chapter in this section focuses on how to build an attribute list. By turning the lens towards the category buyer, we can draw on knowledge about how buyers use attributes to buy brands to inform the most useful types of attributes to track.

A note on terminology: *attributes*, *associations* and *perceptions* are all examples of largely interchangeable terms that refer to the information that could be attached to the brand name in buyer memory and be part of the brand's mental image. Throughout this book I am going to use the term *attribute*—defined as *a quality or feature regarded as a characteristic or inherent part of something or someone*—to cover all these terms, and then draw on specific labels such as Category Entry Points (CEPs) or Distinctive Assets to describe any sub-set of attributes with a particular role.

How are brand attributes useful to category buyers?

Ask yourself: *Why do category buyers build up networks of attributes and brands in their memories?*

Think about it … Why bother building brand memories? Why not start every day and every decision with a blank slate? Imagine starting each day with nothing in mind as we decide on what to have for breakfast, what clothing to wear to that important meeting, what to pack the kids for lunch and so on. You are a blank slate, with the whole world before you to discover …

Wait—without memories, such as 'after eating oats you feel a bit healthier', 'that jacket makes you looks more "in charge"' and 'the kids refused to eat the marmalade and Vegemite combination you made for them last week'—it would take forever to get ready in the morning. You would be unlikely to repeat past successes and be doomed to repeat past mistakes.

Our memories allow us to draw on past experiences to engage in subsequent, similar behaviours more efficiently. Our memories allow us to save time by drawing on our recollection of the past. Therefore, our memories are very useful when they tackle commonly encountered contexts. We can then save the hard 'thinking' and external searching for truly unknown or risky situations.

However, even in these rarer, riskier contexts we still need our memories to kick off the process—to know what to (re)search. Before we enter anything into our search engine of choice, our memory has activated its own internal search to give us ideas for what to type or say.

Memories always matter. Even in front of a physical shelf or when viewing a screen full of products, we do not take the time to look at everything (Anesbury et al. 2016). Our memories naturally narrow our attention from the *many available* to a *select few* that are known and possibly useful. Building brand memories in the minds of category buyers improves the odds of the brand surviving this filtering process.

Building networks of brand memories

Every day you experience the world. Think about yesterday and remember your interactions with brands. You might remember the brand of your morning coffee, the brand of your breakfast cereal, the brand of car you drove to work, the brand of the food outlet where you bought lunch and so on. These are 'brand-memory building' moments, as your ability to remember these experiences means you were sufficiently attentive in the moment for the brand encounter to noticeably affect your memory (see Figure 3.1).

If we also followed you with a camera yesterday, the images will show some brand encounters you noticed but do not remember. These 'in-situ attention only' moments, often stimulated by the environment, get the attention of your memory at the time, but do not get processed into your longer-term memory. For example, in shopper studies that ask people in a supermarket the price of an item straight after putting it into their trolley/basket, 50% are unable to name the price within +/–5% a mere five seconds after purchase (e.g., Dickson and Sawyer 1990). That lack of specific price recall does not mean price was irrelevant to the choice. The shopper may have noticed the price in the moment, but they did not process it enough to build a sufficiently strong long-term memory to retrieve the price at a later point in time.

That same camera would also capture a range of brand encounters you did not notice on any conscious level. The brand of tea sitting next to the coffee, that billboard on the highway, the food outlet next door to the one you walked into. These interactions do not directly impact our memories but can still be captured by our automatic frequency processing mechanism (Hasher and Zacks 1984). This exposure can unconsciously feed into our sense of familiarity/liking (in line with 'mere exposure effects' as per Zajonc 1968), but it is unclear how these unconsciously recorded interactions affect the brand's links to specific attributes. This effect is better treated as a bonus rather than as an objective.

Figure 3.1: Brand exposure moments

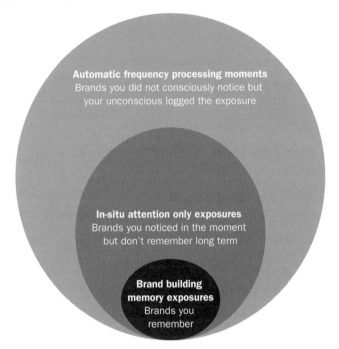

Brand-memory building moments are hard to create

Of the many types of interactions, it is no surprise that the brand-memory exposures you remember are better at refreshing and building the brand's network of attributes than the ones you do not remember. That leads to the obvious conclusion that marketers should aim for more of these types of interactions. The challenge with achieving this objective is people have lives outside of brands.

Brands, as a general experience, are only a small part of a category buyer's life, and most specific brands are only a minuscule part of the fabric of any category buyer's day, week, month or year. Think about a brand you buy and try to recount how much time you spent thinking about it in the last week (thinking that was about the brand, not the product).

Wasn't much was it? And that is a brand you buy.

Now for a real challenge: think about a brand you don't buy and try to remember how much time you spent thinking about it in the last week. Now repeat that process for another brand in the same category that you don't buy. It's hard to even think of the brands, isn't it?

Welcome to the challenges of building memories, particularly among light and non-buyers. Even for a product we use a lot (say like our mobile phones), we rarely think about the brand of phone as we are too busy thinking about other things. Category buyers' time spent thinking about brands is limited and most of this occurs when buying or using brands. This reinforces the status quo; that is, our existing brand buying patterns.

It is only if we are in an unusual situation that we might venture out of the status quo and actively look for something else. If I am having a vegan over for dinner, I might re-examine my dessert options to check these options would suit a vegan and, if not, seek a vegan alternative. But if it is just my non-vegan friends, then I know a cheesecake is always going to work, and I have a repertoire of cream cheese, egg, butter and biscuit brands to satisfy my cheesecake-making needs. If I conduct an online search in this buying situation, it is to get a new recipe, not because I am unsure which brand of cream cheese to buy.

A key role of marketing communications is to get category buyers thinking about the brand at times and in places where they would not normally do so. However, these 'out-of-purchase/consumption' moments are limited by two factors:

1 *Money* – Every brand has a limited amount of money to spend in their media budget.

2 *Lack of category buyer motivation* – Buyers do not notice (and do not want to notice) everything that brands do. There is no reason for me to notice everything from every cream cheese brand—what I know about the ones I know is sufficient right now.

These constraints mean you need to wisely use any category buyer attention the brand's marketing activity gains. You are not going to have an unfettered opportunity to build every possible attribute, so you will need to prioritise. To help with the prioritisation process, we can explore the role of brand memories in buying situations.

Which brand memories are useful for buyers?

I like the word *useful* when it comes to branding. It appeals to my practical nature—it is not as highfaluting as 'purpose' or as imperious as 'driver', but about being of help. A brand memory is useful to the buyer if it is likely to be helpful in buying situations. An attribute's usefulness to the buyer makes it also a useful link for the brand to build in buyer memory, so that when a buyer uses the attribute, the brand is also memorable.

When you host a party, you think about what guests will want to drink, and buy those beverages in advance so when people turn up, you can provide them with a drink they will want. Similarly, when building a brand, think about the attributes that buyers will likely use when buying and create fresh links between those attributes and the brand prior to buying. Your marketing activities can then provide the opportunities for buyers to create and freshen links for those attributes to your brand.[1]

Three key buying roles for attributes

The usual outcome of most buying situations is one brand is bought. Life would be simple (albeit boring) if there was just one option to buy in each category. In the real world, however:

- in every category there are many, many options, many of which are perfectly fine to buy
- in most buying situations people want to move quickly and easily from generating a category need to satisfying this need.[2]

How do buyers get from *the many possible* to *the one choice* with as little time and effort as possible? Here we will focus on three key roles that attributes can play.

---

[1] Note the reverse does not really work—advertising an attribute will not automatically make it useful to the buyer. For example, a while back some milk brands advertised about the type of *casein* in their brands. I am sure even the few people who paid attention to this when it was advertised have forgotten this now.

[2] Now I can hear the collective push-back thinking of buying situations that are outside this common paradigm—please hold onto that thought and allow me to first deal with common buying contexts. I am not dismissing buying outside of this common model, but the most common model is the reference point that becomes the baseline to compare other buying contexts. It is important to understand the common, so we can know what is exceptional.

Role 1: Evoke suitable options from memory

I think, therefore I am said Descartes, and *I evoke, therefore I could buy* would be the Mental Availability equivalent. Getting the brand thought of a specific buying occasion is a useful first step to purchase. This first step was originally conceived as the getting into the 'consideration set', which is the progeny of Brand Awareness and brand attitude.

The consideration set is treated like a popular nightclub that brands want to enter so they can be available when category buyers visit to find 'the one' (for the night at least!). In this analogy, Brand Awareness is the promoter getting brands to queue outside to want to be in the nightclub and brand attitude is the bouncer only letting in the 'most attractive' brands through the door. In each choice situation, a category buyer selects among the brands in the nightclub. If a brand is badly behaved or no longer an attractive potential mate, it gets kicked out of the nightclub and replaced by a more attractive alternative. Meanwhile, non-considered brands try to make themselves look 'attractive' enough to get the bouncer's attention (such as through advertising, social media) and be let inside too.

The problem with this analogy is that it neglects the inherent variability of memory retrieval. There is no set of brands that always gets into the nightclub.

Brands retrieved can vary when buyers use different retrieval cues

A retrieval cue is any idea that someone uses to access information from their memory. For example, if I know I will have a week off in Europe I might think of 'cities in Europe with good food to hang out for a week' and this brings to mind a set of destinations that fit that criteria ('a city', 'in Europe', 'good food' and 'for a week') such as (as I write this) Lisbon, Athens, Madrid, Bologna and Naples.

Retrieval cues come from the contexts that buyers experience. CEPs represent the characteristics of these contexts that influence brand retrieval at the moment when a person enters into the state of being a 'category buyer'.[3] Most of the time most people are *not* buyers for any one category.

---

3   Thanks to Chad Wollen who provided the inspiration for this name during a project we were
     involved with when he was at AOL—more years ago than either of us would want to admit!

Then something happens, and a switch is flicked for someone to transition from 'normal mode' to 'category buyer mode'. CEPs are the thoughts that flick that switch and act as retrieval cues to shape the memories for brands that flow immediately after.

Over buying occasions, rarely do buyers enter a category via only one context. To illustrate this, Table 3.1 shows the figures across 50 CEP studies conducted by the Ehrenberg-Bass Institute in nine different category types. On average only 14% of category buyers encountered only one CEP in the time frame of measurement (ranging from one week to 12 months). This was slightly higher in beverages (21%) and slightly lower in kids' products (6%).

The average number of CEPs that buyers experienced across these studies is 6.4. This average is slightly higher in kids' products (9.3) and snacks (8.2), and slightly lower in services and food products (both 5.4). Category buyers that only used one CEP in the period were also around twice as likely to be light category buyers, which suggests using one CEP is at least partially due to lack of buying opportunities.

Table 3.1 shows us that most category buyers use multiple CEPs to enter the category. Therefore, it is valuable for a brand to have links to multiple CEPs, rather than just one.

Table 3.1: Average number of CEPs and sole CEP % across categories

Category type	Number of studies	Time frames	Mean number of CEPs	% only using one CEP
Household	7	12 months	6.1	11
Personal care	9	3–12 months	5.9	15
Beverages	6	1–3 months	5.3	21
Food	7	1–6 months	5.4	19
Snacks	5	1–3 months	8.2	12
Services	5	6–12 months	5.4	10
OTC	5	1–12 months	7.4	17
Kids' products	3	1 week to 1 month	9.3	6
Retail	3	1–12 months	4.2	18
Average			**6.4**	**14**

When retrieval cues vary, often so do the brands that come to mind. We see this in the brand's category buyers link to different cues (Ratneshwar and Shocker 1991, Holden and Lutz 1992, Desai and Hoyer 2000). Table 3.2 shows an example from social media from *How Brands Grow Part 2* (Romaniuk 2021b, p. 71).

Table 3.2: Example of cue response variability for social media category

CEP	Female 55–70 years Arizona	Female 16–24 years New York	Male 25–34 years West Virginia	Male 45–54 years Florida
Good to use in the evening before bed	Facebook Messenger Instagram YouTube	Facebook YouTube	None	WhatsApp
When someone wants quick and instant response	Facebook Messenger Instagram YouTube	Messenger WhatsApp	Twitter	Twitter
Something to do while watching TV or eating	Facebook Messenger Instagram YouTube	Instagram	Pinterest YouTube	Instagram Snapchat Twitter WhatsApp
For someone who wants to keep up with news/ current events	Facebook Messenger Instagram YouTube	Facebook Messenger Instagram WhatsApp	LinkedIn Twitter	Twitter YouTube

The brands retrieved can vary even when the same cue is reused

When the same person repeatedly uses the same cue, the set of brands retrieved *in each moment* can change. We see this when the same people are re-interviewed and asked the same questions about brand-attribute links at a later point in time. Responses are neither 100% stable, nor random—the second wave of responses vary predictably, in line with the idea of probabilistic retrieval from memory (Dall'Olmo Riley et al. 1997, Sharp 2002, Rungie et al. 2005).

Table 3.3 shows an example of this pattern again from social media network and messaging sites. The Wave 1 (W1) scores for each brand are in the first column and in the second column is the repeat rate—the percentage of W1 responders that repeated the response in Wave 2 (W2).

The results show the average repeat rate is around 50%, with the repeat rate correlated with the initial response level.[4] As with Brand Awareness responses in Chapter 2, re-retrieval of the brand, even for the same attribute, is always uncertain (much lower than 100% repeat rate) but is more likely for bigger brands on more common associations.

Table 3.3: Stability of social media perceptions, United States

Something to do while watching TV or eating	Response level W1	Repeat rate W2
Facebook	65	85
YouTube	29	60
Instagram	29	56
Twitter	29	63
Pinterest	19	48
Facebook Messenger	16	31
Snapchat	14	58
Reddit	11	47
WhatsApp	8	38
TikTok	7	30
LinkedIn	7	36
Vevo	5	38
Average	**20**	**49**

n=208 social media users in the United States, 12 months between interviews

These two types of variability again reinforce the idea that buyers have many evoked sets comprising of lists of brands tailored to meet each moment, rather than a single, stable set of brands to choose from on each occasion. Retrieval at a single point in time is dependent on having a link to the retrieval cue at that time, but also contingent on the freshness of that link relative to competitor options, as well as having the probability goddesses on your brand's side. Anything with a link to the retrieval cue can possibly be retrieved, no matter how tenuous that link. An example of this is when you suddenly think of that chocolate bar you haven't eaten in

---

4   For these two attributes, the Pearson's correlation is 89%, p<0.05.

ages (hello Bounty!)—that is a low retrieval probability item that suddenly gets its short-lived spot in the sun.

In the long run, the brand's propensity to be retrieved, or its Mental Availability, depends on how wide and how fresh its network is across those likely retrieval cues in buying situations, or CEPs.

CEPs come from the category buyer's internal environment (needs, motivations, current or desired emotional states) or the external environment (where, when, who you are with). There will be more on CEPs and Mental Availability measurement in Chapters 5 and 6.

Role 2: Evaluate multiple, mentally equivalent, options

Sometimes only one option comes to mind, and that option is good enough, so the buyer buys and moves on with their life. However, often multiple options are evoked—what then? The buyer has a choice to make. This leads to the question: *Which one to buy when there is a Mental Availability tie?* Sometimes Physical Availability is the decider (see Chapter 14): one is easier to buy than the others and so gets the gig. In this case no more attribute-thinking is needed.

On occasion other attributes can play a role to help the category buyer decide between mentally available brands. The following are some examples of other common attribute types.

Baseline category competencies

In each category you can identify the qualities needed to be an acceptable brand and these can be represented as attributes. Examples include *trustworthy*, *reliable* and *good quality*. Baseline competencies are the qualities where a brand needs to have a minimum level to be a suitable option in the category. These factors are more notable in omission than commission, as doubts about performance can lead someone to reject the brand as an option.

For example, I perceive car brands to be reliable in general (e.g., all start up when you activate the ignition and can get me from A to B), but if I have doubts about Tesla's reliability due to hearing about another of its models being recalled due to a fault, then I might reject Tesla based on my perception that the brand lacks reliability. I do not buy the most reliable car brand, but I will not buy a car brand I think is unreliable.

When it comes to researching baseline competencies, any deficits can indicate a potential problem with the brand. There are several approaches for detecting brand deficiencies, such as:

- controlling for brand size and category prototypicality and looking for where the brand scores substantively lower than expected (see messaging analysis in Chapter 7)
- looking for reasons behind spikes in brand rejection or customer complaints (see Brand Rejection analysis in Chapter 8).

Corporate social responsibility attributes

Corporate social responsibility includes attributes such as *cares for the environment* or *supports the community* that aim to capture knowledge of the company's activities in the social, environmental and community space. These attributes may become baseline competencies over time or even a potential CEP, but do not assume these attributes have high relevance to category buyers unless there is empirical evidence.

Note: It is possible to test the impact of specific corporate social responsibility marketing activities the brand undertakes without needing an attribute. If you draw on a process akin to assessing advertising reach and impact (as described in Chapter 11), you can test if these activities have reached category buyers, are correctly branded and generate useful messages.

Self-expression/identity attributes

Self-expression/identity includes attributes such as *is the brand for me, is it a brand that understands people like me*, and *is it a brand that fits my image*, which are remnants of the 1980s emphasis on the brand as a form of self-expression, with a sprinkle of brand relationship research from the 1990s. Researchers claimed that buyers were pre-disposed to buying brands whose image matched one's perceived self, or ideal self, or some other self (e.g., Sirgy 1985). Therefore, brand images need to reflect how consumers see themselves (actual) or might want to see themselves (aspirational). These are of questionable value as the theory only works if a brand can identify a sub-set of attributes to reflect the selves that a large enough group of buyers are using brands in the category to represent. Similarly, brand relationship research claimed we form relationships with brands (Fournier 1998) and so some attributes try to capture this relationship.

Personality traits attributes

Borrowed from psychology, personality traits include attributes often draw from Jennifer Aaker's brand personality framework (Aaker 1997). Characteristics include *friendly, fun, down-to-earth, masculine, charming, sporty* or *intelligent.* These are often reflections of advertising creative style, and so are better included as part of an advertising evaluation. You might find it useful to read the research that calls into question the value of brand personality before embarking too far down this path (or to find your way back if you are already lost) (Avis 2012, Avis et al. 2012, Romaniuk and Ehrenberg 2012, Avis and Aitken 2015).

Marketing performance attributes

Marketing performance includes attributes that ask category buyers to judge a brand on specific performance qualities, including *is different from other brands* and *is a leader.* These are not specific associations held by category buyers but are on-the-spot judgements they create in answer to a question. Unless you know why the judgement is made (e.g., why is the brand a leader or why is another brand not a leader?), these are of little value to track as attributes because the actions you need to take to change the brand's score, or that will result from a change in the brand's score, are unclear.

Heuristics

Buyers can also use heuristics to break any Mental Availability ties. Heuristics are simple general decision rules, or mental short cuts, that category buyers can use to act quickly, without the need for much thought (e.g., Kahneman et al. 1982). Examples of heuristics to select between brands in buying contexts include *the closest one, the cheapest one* or *haven't had that one for a while.* These heuristics can be included as attributes, but the ability for a brand to fulfil their requirements changes over buyers and time, due to many individual factors outside of the brand's control.

This complicates any interpretation of attribute responses, and diminishes your ability to take actions, whatever the results.

For example, retrieval for *something new to give the kids* is dependent on what has been previously bought, while *the cheapest one* is dependent on the assortment of items in store, including any current price promotions. Yes, a brand can take advantage of heuristics by knowing which are commonly used and creating portfolio options that might suit, but you still need the Mental Availability to be in the race, even when the heuristic helps make the choice. Therefore, heuristics can be important to research, but add little value to an attribute list in a category buyer memory (CBM) tracker.

Role 3: Identify a brand

A third role for attributes is to help the category buyer identify the brand in media or sales environments. The attributes under this umbrella are the brand's Distinctive Assets, which are the non-brand-name sensory elements that trigger the brand (Romaniuk 2018a). Examples of Distinctive Asset types include colours, logos, characters, fonts or taglines.

The primary role of a Distinctive Asset is to act as a trigger for the brand from category buyer memory when the brand name is not present or not noticed. As Distinctive Assets face mental competition and memory decay, there is a continual battle to keep the link between the Distinctive Asset and the brand name fresh and avoid retrieval failure. Therefore, asset building activities to improve/maintain fame and uniqueness metrics are a necessary part of a Distinctive Asset Management System (as described in Romaniuk 2018b).

A CBM tracker can include the Distinctive Assets that the brand wants to build or protect. However, given the complexity of identifying the assets that are the best options for long-term development, we recommend that the strategic piece to determine which assets to build be done outside of the tracker environment. Once the set of assets that comprise the brand's Distinctive Asset palette has been determined (as per Romaniuk 2018c), you will have a much smaller list of assets to track over time. The limitations of attributes proxies for Distinctive Asset roles such as *standing out on shelf* or *distinctive from other brands* are discussed in Chapter 14 on Physical Availability.

Compiling the attribute list

You can draw from the different attribute roles to create an attribute list for your category.

In the interests of collecting relevant information, but not taxing the category buyer too much with overly large batteries of attributes, start from following attribute mix (see Figure 3.2):

- *CEPs* – Given the importance of Mental Availability in getting the brand bought, a good rule of thumb is to have at least 60–70% of the attributes fit into this category.

- *Baseline competencies* – Identify the factors relevant to be an acceptable member of the category to ensure the brand does not underperform. These attributes should comprise no more than 30% of the attributes in the list.

- *Other attributes* – Aspects such as corporate social responsibility or environmental qualities might be useful for secondary purposes. These attributes should be limited to no more than 20% of the list.

So, for every ten attributes, you should have at least six or seven CEPs, and if you want to do so, divide the remaining three or four between baseline category competencies and other attributes. That ensures your attribute list focuses mainly on useful mental structures but can also satisfy other research interests. Do remember *design for the category*. You should create an attribute list that any brand in the category would want to use, to ensure it has longevity beyond any short-term company priorities.

Figure 3.2: Suggested distribution of attributes across roles

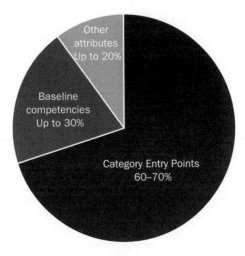

Should this be an attribute?

I have seen some strange things included as attributes in brand health tracking questionnaires. Many reflect marketing fads of the time and quickly become out of date. Invariably new fads emerge, and you will be faced with ideas for new attributes. Mindful that it is easier to start than stop tracking an attribute, here are two questions to ask before deciding to include a new attribute.

Q1. Where would a category buyer learn this link to the brand?

If you cannot trace the source for memory formation (e.g., advertising, social media, packaging), then someone expressing a link either created that association on the spot or it is a halo effect from something else. This will be difficult to effect or action.

For example, the attribute *hard to resist* has popped up in a few questionnaires. Where would someone develop this link? It was not present in any marketing communications or on any packs. Perhaps people could come to that conclusion if the brand was really good at what it delivered—but that means it comes from the evaluation of the experience. As such it is unlikely to be formed prior to usage and be a factor in getting more buyers.

Q2. How would a buyer use this information when buying?

Ask yourself, how might someone who has this attribute present in memory, use this brand memory? Take a realistic audit of the attribute's likely role. Is it something that could be used to evoke brands and be a CEP or something that is more likely to be something used to evaluate brands that are mentally and physically equivalent?

Going back to a previous example, if we improved the brand's link with *hard to resist*, would that translate into more sales?

- Can you imagine someone using this attribute to evoke brands to buy, such as thinking 'I want a pasta sauce, that is *hard to resist'* or an insurance company that is *hard to resist?*
- Could the attribute be used to evaluate brands such as someone looking at two or three pasta sauces and thinking 'that one is *hard to resist'* and choosing the brand based on that assessment?

If there is no clear use case for the attribute in buying, then how would the brand benefit from improvements to this attribute? It is good to be a bit brutal here as most lists of attributes are unnecessarily long. Be wary of overweighting your attribute list with qualities that bear little impact on the choices of most buyers. This just bloats your attribute list and risks the marketing team giving unimportant attributes more attention than they deserve.

What about negatively worded attributes?

Negatively worded attributes (e.g., *poor quality*, *does not deliver on promises*) typically follow different underlying patterns than non-negatively worded attributes. Former buyers have the highest propensity to give a response, followed by brand buyers, with non-buyers the least likely to give a response (Winchester and Romaniuk 2003, Winchester and Romaniuk 2008). However, these negative perceptions are formed after leaving the brand (Winchester et al. 2008). This suggests these negative thoughts are a post-hoc rationalisation developed after leaving the brand to justify the prior behaviour, rather than drivers of brand defection.

That negative perceptions are low among the brand's non-buyers suggests these attributes do not provide insight into why non-buyers do not buy the brand. Therefore, there is little value in tracking negative attributes.

Chapter summary

This chapter covered why we track attributes and three important roles that attributes can play for buyers when buying. The three roles are:

1 *Evoking the brand* – CEPs that help the brand be mentally available.
2 *Evaluating the brand* – Qualities that can be used to evaluate brands when multiple brands have equivalent Mental and Physical Availability.
3 *Identifying the brand* – Distinctive Assets that trigger the brand in media and sales environments.

As a rule of thumb, go for 60–70% CEPs and 30–40% of baseline category competencies and any other attributes. Only track Distinctive

Assets in the Distinctive Asset palette, but put these in separate measurement sections so you can measure fame and uniqueness metrics (see Chapter 5).

Just because you can doesn't mean you should.

It is very easy to turn something into an attribute, measure it and then draw conclusions from the response. When compiling your attribute list, keep in mind the reason for CBM tracking is not to audit all brand knowledge, but to keep track of the brand's performance among useful brand knowledge among category buyers. Including unimportant attributes causes tracker costs to bloat, adds many more pages to your PowerPoint deck, and risks distracting the audience for the report from the important findings.

In the next chapter we will focus on brand attribute measurement.

4

Brand Attributes: Measurement

JENNI ROMANIUK

Attribute measurement should consider the role of the attribute in category buyer choice processes (as discussed in Chapter 3), the unusual context of completing a survey and, of course, the priorities based on the Laws of Growth (from Chapter 1). This chapter examines these influences on three areas integral to brand-attribute measurement:

1 *The attributes* – how should they be worded?
2 *The brands* – do you provide a list or not?
3 *The link between the attributes and brands* – how to measure this relationship?

It also highlights decisions that will impact the ability of a tracker to capture brand memories, particularly from the key audience for growth—the brand's very light/non-buyers.

The attributes

A rose, by any name, might smell as sweet, but Shakespeare should be grateful he did not have to sit in a meeting where the hot topic of discussion is whether *modern* and *up to date* have the same meaning. The process of constructing the attribute list can involve everyone in some frustrating conversations about how to word each attribute quality.

You want an attribute to reflect the value the product delivers versus its price—but which words to use? Is it *good value*? Or *value for money*? Or *worth paying more for*? Or *better value than other brands*? Or just *cheaper*? Oh wait, is *cheaper* something negative? Perhaps it makes people think *cheap and nasty* in which case it is bad … at this point you reach for the nearest (not necessarily the cheapest) gin and tonic!

Does the specific wording of the attribute matter? Maybe it's just an issue of not dwelling on semantics but having a thesaurus close to keep life interesting! However, it turns out the words you put in an attribute can make a substantive difference to the responses that category buyers generate. This next section shows how you can improve the quality of your attribute data by avoiding certain wording styles.

Attribute wording approaches

The base word or phrase to describe an idea is the *general* form (e.g., *innovative*). While the *general* form is the core idea in its simplest form, often in brand health surveys additional words can alter the meaning; for example, *the most innovative brand,* whereby the addition of 'the most' changes the brand's qualifying requirements.

There are three types of modifiers commonly used in tracker attribute lists:

1 *Stronger form* – This is when the attribute includes adverbs such as 'very' or 'more' (e.g., *very innovative*) to indicate that the brand needs a substantial amount of that quality to qualify as linked.

2 *Superlative form* – This is when the attribute is modified to an extreme form, such as *is the best at innovation* or *is the most innovative brand.* In this instance, it is necessary for a brand to be perceived to have extremely high or even the highest performance on the attribute to qualify.

3 *Comparative form* – This is when the attribute asks category buyers to compare the brand to competitors, such as *is more innovative than other brands.* This approach originates from a differentiation mindset, which assumes that category buyers look to buy brands that are better than competitors.

Unfortunately, these modified wording forms act like a filter and suppress responses, particularly from the brand's very light/non-buyers. This filtering process hampers our ability to measure the brand's current performance on that attribute.

Let us look at the results from a test conducted across seven commonly tracked attributes (see Table 4.1). This test compared the responses category buyers gave to the general form[1] to the three modified forms for brands in the quick service food category. Quick service food is a broad category that allows us to test a wide range of attributes across brands of different market shares.

Table 4.1: The wording across the different attribute forms

General form	Stronger form	Comparative form	Superlative form
Is a trustworthy brand	Is a very trustworthy brand	Is more trustworthy than other brands	Is the brand I trust the most
Is good value for money	Is very good value for money	Is better value for money than other brands	Is the best value for money brand
Is good quality	Is excellent quality	Is better quality than other brands	Is the best quality brand
Is a healthy brand	Is a healthier option	Is healthier than other brands	Is the healthiest option
Provides good service	Provides excellent service	Provides better service than other brands	Offers the best service
Innovative	Very innovative	More innovative than other brands	Is the most innovative brand
Good for all the family	Excellent for all the family	Better for all the family than other brands	Is the best option for all of the family

Method

The order in which attributes were presented to respondents was randomised across four different, but equivalent, samples of around 300 category buyers. In all tests, respondents were provided with the

---

1   Note: *good value for money* is technically an adapted form, with value for money a more general form, but *good value for money* is the most typically used general form in trackers and as it is only a mild modifier it was kept as this wording.

same 13 brands in a randomised list. Each respondent only saw one version of each attribute. Respondents' brand buying was also collected so we could classify category buyers into brand buyers and very light/non-buyers.

Results

We compared the number of brands elicited for the general form to the number of brands for the same attribute in modified forms. The results show all three modified forms result in fewer brands being linked to the attribute than the general form. The overall averages in brand-attribute links are lower by:

- 8% for *stronger form*
- 21% for *superlative form*
- 28% for *comparative form*.

    Several conditions experienced a larger decline in brand responses (see Table 4.2):

- Brand non-buyers' responses declined twice that of buyers (–27% versus –14%).
- Medium and smaller brands suffer more than bigger brands (–24% and –23% versus –16%), particularly for the stronger or superlative wording forms.

Table 4.2: Declines in brand responses for modified attribute forms by brand buying and brand size

	Stronger form %	Superlative form %	Comparative form %	Average
Brand non-buyers	–13	–39	–30	**–27**
Brand buyers	–8	–17	–18	**–14**
Brand size				
Bigger brands (30%+ pen)	–5	–16	–27	**–16**
Medium brands (10–29% pen)	–11	–28	–32	**–24**
Smaller brands (<10% pen)	–10	–26	–32	**–23**

Quick service food data (total n=1,224)

Why lower responses for attributes with modified wording?

The responses are lower for the modifications because the modified attributes invite category buyers to undertake a two-step cognitive process:

1 To think of brands linked to the attribute.
2 To select responses from this sub-set based on the modification, such as which brand is 'very', which one is 'the best', and which one is 'better than others'.

While all buyers undertake the same process and all brands must overcome these two hurdles to be linked to any attribute, it is more difficult for some.

Smaller brand responses suffer more than bigger brand responses

Bigger brands monopolise light category buyers (Dawes 2020, Sharp and Romaniuk 2021a). Lighter category buyers often only know the bigger brands, which means these brands compete with few, if any, other brands for initial retrieval or subsequent selection. Therefore, modifications only have a minor effect on bigger brand response levels. However, buyers of smaller brands tend to be heavier category buyers. These heavy category buyers usually also buy the bigger brands, so the smaller brands in these buyers' repertoires compete against bigger brands in both retrieval and selection steps. This means that a smaller brand has a lower chance than a bigger brand of being linked to a modified attribute, even among its own buyers.

Very light/non-buyer responses suffer more than buyer responses

For all attributes, brand buyers have higher propensity to link a brand than non-buyers (Bird et al. 1970, Romaniuk, Bogomolova et al. 2012). Therefore, non-buyers are more likely to fall at the first step/hurdle. However, even if a non-buyer makes it through the first hurdle, the chance of any brand not experienced/used successfully meeting the second criterion of excellent, superior, or better than other brands in memory is very low. This means that very light/non-buyers are less likely to respond when attributes are modified in any of these three ways.

Do you want a smaller, biased set of brand responses?

These modified forms of attribute wording cause respondents to link fewer brands to attributes. The omissions are not random but tend to be concentrated in the crucial segment of very light/non-buyers and disproportionately impact the responses smaller brands gain.

Whether your brand is bigger or smaller, biased data is not helpful:

- *For managers of bigger brands* – You get an unduly 'rosy' view of your own brand's performance and a reduced ability to detect competitive threats early.
- *For managers of smaller brands* – You get an unduly negative view of the brand's current performance relative to bigger competitors, and risk stopping effective marketing activity due to this misinterpretation.

Therefore, it is sensible to avoid these modifications if you want to get a more complete, unbiased view of brand associations in category buyer memory. The *general form* is the recommended option for any attribute wording.

The brands

Life would be easier if we did not need to prompt for brands. There would be no need to make decisions about what to include, and no risk of missing an important brand or inflating scores for an obscure brand that happened to make the list. We could just get the unfiltered responses from category buyers.

The interest in Mental Availability, which is about brands 'coming to mind' in buying situations, has further ignited the interest in unprompted measurement of brand/attribute links. Many a researcher (including me) has assumed that as in the real-world category buyers rely on unprompted elicitation of the brand, then Mental Availability measures should mirror this approach.

However, the empirical evidence on unprompted brand attribute measurement tells a familiar cautionary story that refutes this assumption. Relying on unprompted approaches for brand responses creates biases against brand non-buyers and depresses the relative scores for smaller brands. To understand why this happens, let us look again into the fundamentals of memory retrieval.

Remember the basics of memory retrieval

In Chapter 2, retrieval from memory is described as a 'cue-activation' process. A cue is the entry point to memory (e.g., *something to cool me down*) and anything connected to that cue can be retrieved (e.g., a Coke, Sprite, Lipton iced tea). However, each retrieval occasion has a finite amount of 'activation' to expend, and an unprompted approach uses a lot of this activation on the first one or two retrievals. This means that fewer brands can jump the hurdle from long-term memory into what is commonly referred to as 'working memory'.

We saw this in Brand Awareness measures (Chapter 2). We can also see this in empirical tests that compare the brand-attribute responses from samples of category buyers who are prompted for brands with category buyers answering for the same attributes but without brand names. Category buyers link more brands to attributes when provided with brand lists. For example, across 12 attributes in the mobile phone handset category, the average number of brand linkages is around two-thirds higher when brand names are provided (24.4 versus 14.7 attributes, only counting brands also on the prompted list).

But is more better? One aspect of unprompted measurement is that it could uncover brands that would be missed if you confined responses to a brand list. However, if we expand the brand count to any mobile phone brand in our unprompted test, the average is only slightly higher (15.9 brand responses). Therefore, you might miss a few brand linkages when you provide category buyers with a list, but you miss many more by not providing the list.

As a side note, I have tried putting an open-ended 'Other' option in the brand list to capture 'out of list' responses, but respondents rarely used this feature. Omissions are best reduced with a well-constructed brand list, which is covered later in the chapter.

The real world versus the survey world

Our lives (thankfully) differ considerably from a market research survey.

In the real world we do just one retrieval from memory from a category at a time. I need a quick lunch today, so I use that cue and get the options and then progress quickly to buying and eating lunch. And then I move on with my life. However, in a survey you will ask me about the brands I link to a 'quick lunch' and then a 'healthy lunch' (that was yesterday), and then a 'lunch to give the kids' (which I don't do very often), and then 'something warming on a cold day' (which might be last weekend). The cues I use over a week, month or even a year get condensed into one repeat-measure attribute block.

What happens when you ask multiple, similar, unprompted questions in quick succession? Well, it depends on the type of category.

In a category where the typical buyer buys multiple brands over a period, such as toothpaste, beer or TV streaming services, category buyers retrieve *some* brands linked to the first attribute cue. These brands *are* usually not all brands known in that category, it is not even all brands linked to that particular attribute (remember same cue retrieval variability from Chapter 3), but *some of them*. After that first retrieval, these brands then hang around in a category buyer's working memory, which is where we store our last retrieved items.

When that same person is then asked about another attribute, why would their brain bother to dig again into long-term memory when some 'easy' brand responses are already in working memory?

The answer is it doesn't. Remember the human brain can be quite lazy …

Its memory draws on the list of brands it already has easily available, and only goes back into long-term memory if it is necessary to complete the task. As the respondent cycles through the attribute list, the chance of an as-yet-unretrieved brand getting a retrieved brand diminishes, and this list of unretrieved brands skews to small brands and/or brands they do not buy.

For example, in Romaniuk (2006), testing in the toothpaste category shows that the gap between the number of brands prompted versus unprompted nearly doubled from 21% to 37% over the course of 20 attributes. As more attributes are measured, unprompted measures miss more responses.

However, for markets where one brand dominates a person's buying, such as insurance or telecommunications, typically the first retrieval is hard work for the category buyer's memory. Only a few brands come to mind for the initial attributes, and these are often not enough to fill up working memory. As more attributes are asked, more brands enter a category buyer's working memory and have a greater opportunity to be linked to these later attributes. Therefore, in a market when buyers tend to subscribe to only one brand, a small brand's chance of retrieval increases as the category buyer moves through the attribute set.

Again, from Romaniuk (2006), over the first four attributes in the insurance category, prompting for brands generates 48% more brands; while for the last four attributes, prompting for brands generates only 10% more brands. The gap between prompted and unprompted brand responses shrinks as category buyers 'warm up' memory for retrieval.

This again highlights how unprompted measurement approaches, by virtue of being more unstable and prone to external influences on retrieval, have more variable response patterns across attributes and category types. But wait, there's more …

Non-buyers and small brands suffer (again)

In both repertoire and subscription markets, the most affected groups were non-buyers and smaller brands. Figure 4.1 illustrates this from the mobile phone handset category in a split sample test involving 12 attributes across three measures: one prompted and two unprompted measures. The latter comprised Unprompted, which is all brands retrieved, and Top-of-Mind (TOM), which is the first brand only. In all cases the unprompted approaches resulted in fewer brands being linked to the attributes (hence the negative scores), but the big negative scores are for smaller brands, brand non-buyers and (the harder) TOM measure. For example, non-buyers of small brands under a TOM measurement condition stated only 6% of the linkages achieved with a prompted approach (as scores are 94% lower).

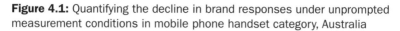
Figure 4.1: Quantifying the decline in brand responses under unprompted measurement conditions in mobile phone handset category, Australia

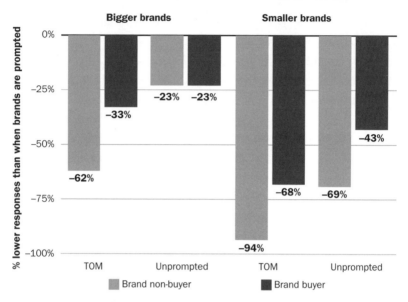

We see that, like Brand Awareness measures (Chapter 2), the more difficult the measure, the more unprompted approaches benefit bigger brands. When looking at the non-buyers of small brands, who are likely to become buyers if that small brand grows, we only see these nascent brand linkages when category buyers are prompted with the brand names.

This means when you don't prompt for brand names:

- the first attribute used to retrieve brands can affect subsequent brand retrievals
- you reduce the chance of getting responses from key growth areas (non-buyers, small brands)
- you risk a distorted view of brand performance, whether bigger (looks better) or smaller (looks worse).

Developing a brand list

This gets us back to that annoying issue of having to develop a brand list. Here are four questions that speak to some of the key concerns researchers have about creating brand lists:

1 Won't category buyers just make up responses because it is easy to just tick any brand?

2 How do I narrow it down to a short list when I have many, many brands in the category?

3 How do I handle variants and private label/retailer brands?

4 What about new launches or deletions?

The following section addresses each of these questions.

Won't category buyers just make up responses because it is easy to just tick any brand?

The good news about brand lists is that, if well-constructed, there is little evidence they encourage category buyers to manufacture brand-attribute links. This is because:

- category buyers can be given over 30 attributes and still have zero linkages to a specific brand
- brand buyer/non-buyer attribute response patterns follow a predictable pattern when brand lists are provided, which would not occur if responses were random/made up.

However, good data quality is not automatic; it relies on having a proper research design that:

- has enough brands so category buyers can feel like they can do their 'job' and answer the question without the need to tick every brand at some point—with only two or three brands, it is easy for someone to notice they have not ticked a specific brand and feel obliged to do so
- makes it easy for someone to say 'none' if they have no brands linked to that attribute by making this an easy to find option on the page
- avoids attributes that lead category buyers towards unknown brands, such as *when I want to try something new/different* (e.g., marketing performance attributes from Chapter 3)
- randomises brand and attribute presentation to redistribute any order effects.

How do I narrow it down to a short list when I have many, many brands in the category?

Your brand list does not need to be a census of all brands. Think of your brand list as covering purchase occasions rather than brands, and that you want to cover as many as possible within the constraints of how many brands you can ask about. This is a 'Goldilocks' number in between two extremes:

1 Too few and you do not cover enough purchase occasions to get a realistic view of the category.

2 Too many and it is too difficult for respondents to find and select brands, so you risk under-representing brand responses.

I prefer to have brand lists that are no more than 20 options, which is feasible with today's online survey designs where brand names are buttons. A lower number might be necessary if mobile phones are the main devices for your data collection. At the other extreme, at least five competitive options help avoid a field sparse enough for someone to notice if they have not linked a brand to any attribute. If your competitor list is very small, then perhaps your category definition is unnecessarily narrow, and does not accurately reflect the competitive field. You can use the analysis that underpins the Duplication of Purchase law (Chapter 1) to examine brand competition patterns in the wider category and check your competitive set matches how people buy, and does not exclude important competitors.

How do I handle private label/retailer brands?

Treating all private labels (PLs) as one category means you will evoke the prototype of the sub-set of PLs rather than any specific linkages for an individual PL brand. Research into the brand equity of PL brands shows that while PLs do often share common prototypically PL qualities (e.g., lower price/good value, but slightly lower quality), individual PLs can deviate from this prototype (e.g., Nenycz-Thiel 2010).

Deviations from the PL prototype occur because retailers execute different PL strategies, particularly:

- different PL tiers causing variations in the perceptions category buyers hold across PL brand portfolios (e.g., premium PLs such as Tesco Finest)
- differences in retailer images that can influence the perceptions category buyers hold of different retailers' PLs (e.g., more upmarket *Costco* and *Kirkland* versus the more discounted *Lidl* and *Preferred Selection*)
- different naming protocols that influence whether category buyers transfer the retailer image to the PL (retailer co-branded like

Sainsbury/Sainsbury Taste the Difference or separate like *Walmart/ Great value* and *Superindo/365*).

Including PLs as one option can blind you to insights to help address the competition from specific PLs offered by specific retailers, particularly if an individual PL has a high share in your category. As a rule, if any individual PL in a specific category (e.g., Walmart's Great Value in the Cream Cheese category) has substantive market share, then this PL brand should have its own slot on the brand list.

If you are in a category where the PL prototype is strong, no single PL has substantive share *but* combined PLs have sufficient share to be of interest as a competitive group, then you can put in a catch-all 'Private Label/Store Brand' response. While this approach has the previously mentioned limitations due to combining multiple brands under one banner, it means you do not totally omit PLs from the survey. However, you should monitor individual retailer PL shares for emerging threats. Every couple of years conduct a separate check on the adherence to PL prototypes, by measuring individual PLs and attributes to check there are no differences of substance between PLs. If the prototypes persist, then all PL brands should score as expected (see Chapter 7).

How do I handle variants?

Brands can have large, complex portfolios with a wide range of variants and sub-brands in the mix. Some variants can have substantive market shares on their own and might need their own 'spot' in the tracker.

Again, we need to balance the desire to be precise with the realities of retrieval. If you include a sub-brand with essentially the same name (e.g., Dolmio and Dolmio Extra), the sub-brand or variants get 'un-entitled' linkages to attributes simply because it shares the core brand name (also referred to as a halo effect; see, for example, Beckwith and Lehmann 1975). If the sub-brand or variant gets most of its linkages due to a halo effect, there is no need to measure it separately—measuring the core brand tells you how it will be perceived.

However, include a core brand's variants or sub-brands if they:

- have a separate marketing budget and their own communication activities

- are building their own brand identity
- have longevity and are not just short-term launches to capitalise on a trend, fad, event or season.

If you do decide to include your brand/portfolio variants, then remember that *designing for the category* means you must apply the same rules to competitors' sub-brands/variants.

What about new launches and deletions?

Inevitably, the list will need updating over time. As a category evolves, new entrants will be launched, and existing brands will be delisted. Deletions are usually easy to remove, as typically these brands perform at a low level and so have little impact on attribute scores.

New entrants are a little more complicated, and, as in most things in life, timing is everything. Do not rush to include all new entrants but leave some time to check they are going to stick around. In packaged goods, around 20% of new launches fail in the first 12 months, and a further 10–15% fail by the end of year two (Victory et al. 2021), so it is useful to wait at least a year to clear out the real duds before making any major changes.

In the interim you do not need to be blind to the performance of these new launches. Use other measures such as prompted awareness (Chapter 2), attitude/rejection questions (Chapter 8) and Presence tracking (Chapter 14) to get an initial sense of a new launch's performance and future trajectory. Growing prompted awareness, continued low rejection rates a year or two after launch, and expanded distribution should signal that the new launch is here to stay and therefore worth adding to the survey. When you add a new brand, some adjustments may be necessary. Chapter 7 covers these.

Guidelines to construct a brand list

When designing the list, remember this part of the maxim—*design for the category*. This means your brand list should include:
- all larger and medium share brands in the category
- individual PL brands that have a substantive share, or 'all PL brands' if individual PLs have low share but PLs in total have a noteworthy total share, and there is strong adherence to the same PL prototype

- a representative sample of small brands, with preference given to those with current or likely above-the-line marketing activity
- of course, your brand(s).

Review your brand list as if you were a medium-sized competitor brand—would you still use the same list? When the answer is yes, you are good to go.

Well-meaning ideas that compromise data quality

We all appreciate the heavy cognitive load that our questionnaires can put on respondents. However, some efforts to make the survey easier for category buyers unintentionally lessen data quality. Here are a few such approaches.

An 'All brands' option

It is tempting to include an 'all of these' button in the brand list to make life easier for respondents. Instead of clicking 20 or so individual brands, respondents can just click one response to express all those responses. This can reduce data quality because of the following reasons:

- An 'All of these' response rarely reflects reality—even when providing all brands in lists of fewer than ten brands, respondents rarely tick all brands. Therefore, with an easy to press 'All of these' button you get 'constructed' responses as category buyers can tick it for convenience when more than half the brands fit the attribute, rather than only when they genuinely link every brand to that attribute. Leaving one or two or even three brands out might not be worth the effort of ticking all the rest.
- An 'all of these' response inflates the scores of all small brands and therefore blunts the measure's sensitivity to detect when there are real changes in attribute links for an individual small brand.

Using prompted Brand Awareness responses to filter brand lists

Another approach to ease the cognitive load on respondents is to reduce the brand list by removing all brands that each individual category buyer did not tick for the prompted Brand Awareness measure.

The following points explain why this reduces data quality:

- It assumes that prompted awareness is a 100% accurate measure, when it is quite easy for respondents to miss a brand or two in a long list. The initial error compounds when prompted awareness is used as the screener for other measures.
- Atypical brands might not be recognised until the right context; for example, Kinder Bueno might not be linked to chocolate category in general but arise from memory for the attribute of *a good option for kids*.
- You can end up in a situation where someone might have only two brands and someone else might have ten brands on their list. This is the same problem as having a list for everyone that contains too few brands. A small list creates pressure to tick every brand at least once.

To avoid these issues, give everyone the same brand list. In a survey, as in life, category buyers can easily screen in some brands and ignore others.

Measuring brand to attribute instead of attribute to brand

When the attribute list is long and the brand list is shorter, it is tempting to flip the question and ask category buyers which attributes they link to each brand. While a brand-cued approach draws from the same part of memory as an attribute-cued approach, respondents only expend so much energy on any one question. As there are usually more attributes linked to a brand than brands linked to an attribute, fewer linkages are retrieved under the brand-to-attribute condition.

A second issue with this approach is that a brand-to-attribute measurement approach heightens responses for small brands and leads more people to give at least one response. This inflates the scores of small brands.

In Figures 4.2 and 4.3, using the mobile phone handset category, we can see these two effects:

1 Big brand responses reduced, as people run out of 'steam' for big brands (around –40% for Samsung Galaxy and Apple iPhone, see Figure 4.2).

2 Small brands get many more people giving at least one attribute response, as category buyers are forced to pay exclusive attention to a

brand that would otherwise get much lower, if any, attention (+60% for HTC, +41% for Xiaomi and +67% for Aspera; see Figure 4.3).

Therefore, the attribute-to-brand approach avoids drawing undue attention to smaller brands and gets a more comprehensive set of memory links than a brand-to-attribute approach.

Figure 4.2: Difference in number of attributes for a brand when attribute-cued versus brand-cued measurement in mobile phone handset brands, Australia

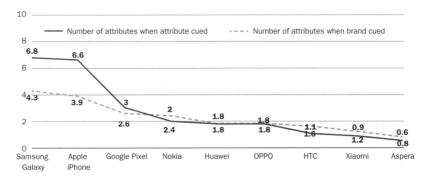

Figure 4.3: Difference in % giving at least one brand-attribute link when attribute-cued versus brand-cued measurement in mobile phone handset brands, Australia

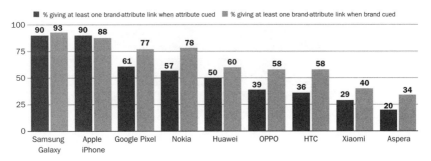

Measuring the link between the attribute and the brand

Once you have the attribute and brand lists, the next issue is how to measure the relationship between the two. In the next section we examine two popular options for measuring brand-attribute relationships: (1) a 'free choice, pick any' approach, or (2) a rating on scales approach.

Free choice, pick any approach

A common approach in commercial market research is a 'free choice, pick any' approach (see Figure 4.4). This approach has the following four characteristics:

1 Category buyers indicate relationship between brands and attributes in a binary format (1 = linked, 0 = no response).
2 The upper limit on the number of brands that category buyers can link to each attribute is the number provided in the brand list.
3 The upper limit on the number of attributes that category buyers can link to each brand is the number of attributes provided.
4 The lower limit for both brands and attributes is zero, with category buyers free to score no brands for any attribute, or no attributes for any brand. Category buyers can even link no brands to any attributes, although in reality this is rare.

Figure 4.4: Example of a free choice, pick any approach layout

This approach measures the attribute's potential as a piece of information that could be a retrieval cue or retrieved when the brand is the cue. Although used in marketing research prior to the integration of memory theory into marketing (e.g., Joyce 1963), the approach is aligned with the Associative Network Theories of Memory (Anderson and Bower 1973). Under this set of theories, memory is treated as a network of linked nodes representing different ideas, with the brand name one node and each attribute another node. The aim of measurement is to establish if there is a link between the attribute and the brand name in category buyer memory, a link that pre-existed measurement and should persist after measurement.

The key advantages of this approach are:

- *face validity* – it mirrors a binary 'retrieved or not' from long-term memory into working memory
- *responses follow a predictable structure* – the data follows systemic patterns that can be used to estimate brand responses on each attribute, which provides a more robust understanding of brand/attribute linkages (e.g., Romaniuk and Sharp 2000, Romaniuk and Huang 2019) (more on this in Chapter 7)
- *greater brand level discrimination* – the results show greater brand level variation than ranking or rating measures (e.g., Barnard and Ehrenberg 1990, Driesener and Romaniuk 2006)
- *greater category coverage* – the ease of response means you can include more brands than with scales, providing a more comprehensive view of the category.

The key disadvantages of this approach are:

- *sample size requirements* – greater sample sizes are needed for statistical significance testing compared to scales
- *lack of individual level discrimination* – a binary approach does not provide any 'degree of' responses, so brands cannot be ordered for an individual category buyer. If someone ticks two brands for *good for kids* it is impossible to tell if one brand is better than the other brand on this quality. We can only tell performance at brand level, such as if more category buyers link a brand to an attribute such as *good for kids,* compared to other brands.

Rating on scales approach

A rating on scales approach is where category buyers rate each brand on each attribute using a multi-point scale (5 or 7-point scale is typical, but there can also be 10 or 11-point scales). The scale design can involve verbal anchors, such as the Likert scale (Likert 1932), which asks people to express how much they agree or disagree with a statement. There can be verbal anchors at all points or just at the extremes and middle (as shown in Figure 4.5).

Figure 4.5: Example of rating scale format

You will next see some statements that people have linked to brands of <insert category>.
Please look at each statement and rate each brand on how well you feel the statement applies.
The scale ranges from Strongly disagree to Strongly agree.

How much do you agree that the brands of mobile phones fit with the following statement?

Something everyone in the family will enjoy

	Strongly disagree			Neither agree nor disagree			Strongly agree
Brand 2	●	●	●	●	●	●	●
Brand 5	●	●	●	●	●	●	●
Brand 8	●	●	●	●	●	●	●
Brand 1	●	●	●	●	●	●	●
Brand 4	●	●	●	●	●	●	●
Brand 3	●	●	●	●	●	●	●
Brand 7	●	●	●	●	●	●	●
Brand 9	●	●	●	●	●	●	●
Brand 6	●	●	●	●	●	●	●

This approach has its roots in cognitive attitude theories, whereby a brand's overall performance is based on its performance for specific qualities/attributes (e.g., Fishbein and Ajzen 1975). There is no evidence that we store attribute information in memory as, for example, '*I strongly agree the brand is good value for money*', which means these evaluations do not exist outside of the question prompt. We just form this opinion when asked (either by others or ourselves).

Rating attributes on scales is particularly popular in academic research. This approach makes multivariate analysis easier, and achieves statistically significant results with smaller sample sizes, making research less expensive. However, while there are ostensibly many different scale points for category buyers to choose, the empirical distributions show that three of these scale points dominate responses—neutral, slightly positive and strongly positive (see Figure 4.6). Very few category buyers use the negative scale points. Therefore, just because you ask category buyers to respond on five or seven scale points, does not mean these extra scale points are necessary or useful.

Figure 4.6: Scale distributions to an attribute for a food product, United Kingdom

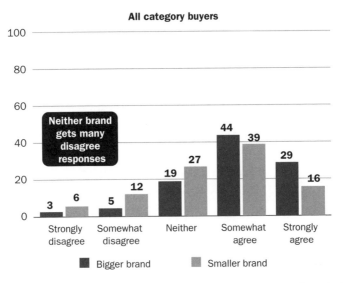

Non-buyers, in the absence of a non-response option, often default to the scale midpoint. For small brands, with lots of non-buyers, this excess at the midpoint inflates the average score, which, in turn, dampens brand level variation (Romaniuk 2008).

Table 4.3 shows an example of the excess in 'neither' from brand very light/non-buyers in the confectionery category. A brand's very light/non-buyers are more likely to say 'neither', and the score is highest for the non-buyers of the smaller brand.

Table 4.3: Average percent of category buyers saying 'neither agree nor disagree' across five attributes, confectionery category

	Brand non-buyers	Brand buyers
Bigger brand	26	15
Smaller brand	31	18

The lack of negative responses means that the opposite of a 'yes' is rarely no; it's more often 'don't know'. If the brand is not good value, it is not poor value; rather, it is just many category buyers, particularly the brand's non-buyers, do not have an opinion.

The midpoint default effect is evident in the relative lack of brand variation in scale mean scores compared to the free choice, pick any approach (see Table 4.4). The free choice, pick any scores range from 42% to 5% (37pp difference), while the average mean scale scores for the same brands on the same attributes are more clustered, ranging from 5.0 to 4.1 (0.9 difference).

Even the smallest brands score higher than the midpoint of 3.5 out of 5, which reflects the distribution of mainly neutral, slightly agree responses. If we convert the raw scores for both approaches into Z-scores, so they can be compared on the same scale, the free choice, pick any approach has nearly three times the variance (+/-0.11 versus 0.4) of scale scores.

Including a 'don't know' option reduces this reliance on the midpoint, but this then creates more 'missing values', which either reduces the sample size available for analysis or corrects by assigning them a value (often the mean, median or mode), which creates the same score inflation issue.

Table 4.4: Example of variation across brands for free choice, pick any versus scales

Responses to 'good value for money'	Free choice, pick any % linkage	5-point Likert scale, mean
Samsung Galaxy	42	5.0
Apple iPhone	27	4.2
Huawei	23	4.4
Nokia	21	4.7
OPPO	20	4.5
Google Pixel	18	4.7
HTC	13	4.4
Xiaomi	12	4.2
Aspera	5	4.1
Average	**20**	**4.5**
Std dev/Std dev for Z-score	**10.5/0.11**	**0.3/0.04**
Range	**37**	**0.9**

The advantages of rating attributes on scales are:

- *sampling efficiency* – low sample size requirements for statistical significance testing between groups

- *analysis flexibility* – some statistical approaches (such as structural equation modelling) are possible/much easier
- *individual level differences* – it is possible to identify if there are any differences between brands at individual buyer level and to pinpoint if one brand is stronger than another for a specific category buyer.

The disadvantages of rating attributes on scales are:

- *hard work for respondents* – this is taxing on respondents as it requires responding specifically to every brand and attribute combination
- *artificial sensitivity* – using a scale can give an inflated impression of sensitivity, as category buyers rarely use negative/disagree response points. It is only a more sensitive measurement if category buyers' evaluations genuinely vary in line with the scale.
- *expense* – scales are lengthier to collect, particularly if you have many brands or attributes. In most academic studies that develop instruments with scales, research participants only evaluate one or two brands, rather than a full category list (e.g., Aaker 1997, Batra et al. 2012). This makes these scaled instruments unwieldy to use in commercial tracking without substantive modification.

Scales are best used when there is true variety in degree of response. For example, when rating the different attributes of a recent service encounter, a number of factors such as the friendliness and speed of an individual staff member could affect the specific score on any day. Brand linkages to attributes in a brand health tracker are not that mutable.

What about approaches that rank brands?

Another option is to get category buyers to rank brands on each attribute. This approach also assumes there is more sensitivity than often really exists. However, the task of ranking is even more difficult because category buyers do not have any reason to pre-develop rankings of brands that are say 5th, 6th or 10th. This means when you ask this in a survey, category buyers are doing this for the first time, and so it is cognitively exhausting and of questionable value.

Attempts to solve this by only asking for the top three and bottom three brands still requires people to organise their brand-attribute linkages in an atypical form. Ranking the bottom three is very difficult because it means a category buyer must have opinions for at least six brands to complete the task. If you are a light category buyer, this is highly unlikely.

A further variation on ranking approaches is the best-worst scale Professor Jordan Louviere developed for use in choice modelling (e.g., Louviere and Woodworth 1991). People indicate the best and worst brand on each attribute. This approach fails to properly capture brand-attribute linkages on two grounds:

1 'The best' is only one response and, like TOM measures, biases towards brands used heavily and against non-buyers and small brands, so it fails the 'key audience' test.

2 People rarely have a worst brand readily memorable, as to do so requires experiencing enough brands to know which is the poorest performer. This response is just a rather clumsy rejection measure.

A best-worst approach has many uses in other fields, but this approach to measuring brand-attribute linkages, as part of a brand health tracker, is heavy on the worst and light on the best.

Chapter summary

The following steps give you the best chance of getting a more complete, unbiased read on the brand-attribute linkages in buyer memory:

1 Use the general form of the attribute, avoiding extreme or comparative modifiers.

2 Use a free choice, pick any approach.

3 Construct the brand list to include all the big brands, medium brands and a representative set of small brands, particularly ones that engage in above-the-line expenditure.

4 Prompt everyone for all brands on the list.

5 Anchor with the attribute and ask which brands are linked to the attribute.

6 Randomise the order of attributes and brand lists.

If you are considering any form of attribute modification, test first. Collect the data to examine the response patterns across brand buyers and non-brand buyers. This will ensure the change in wording does not unintentionally bias the data.

5

Mental Availability and Category Entry Points

JENNI ROMANIUK

This chapter covers the origins of Mental Availability, its role in brand growth and relationship with Category Entry Points (CEPs). We then explore the pros and cons of four approaches to identify CEPs in a category and some tips to get a too-long CEP list to a manageable size.

First, a bit of history ...

Mental Availability is the brand's propensity to be thought of in buying situations (as described in Romaniuk 2021a). This concept arose out of the integration of three insights:

1   The knowledge of how human memory works and the inability of a single cued Brand Awareness measure to capture the full extent of brand retrieval (e.g., Holden and Lutz 1992, Holden 1993, Desai and Hoyer 2000, Romaniuk and Sharp 2004).

2   The empirical evidence that the number of attributes linked to a brand is more strongly related to future buyer behaviour than the link to any single attribute (e.g., Romaniuk 2001, Romaniuk 2003, Romaniuk and Sharp 2003b, Winchester et al. 2008).

3 The desire for a buyer memory metrics model that aligns with the Laws of Growth (e.g., Romaniuk 2013).

We initially referred to this idea as brand salience (e.g., Romaniuk and Sharp 2004), but it became apparent that 'brand salience' was too synonymous with Top-of-Mind (TOM) Brand Awareness. This created problems because marketers and researchers:

- felt brand salience was something familiar and so did not absorb the full implications of this concept
- fell for the logical, but misleading, assumption that if being retrieved is good, being retrieved earlier must be better.; however, the biggest barrier to a brand being bought is being thought of in the first place, not first versus second or third
- assumed the key measurement approach to be TOM Brand Awareness, despite the issues with TOM we first highlighted in Romaniuk and Sharp (2004).

Therefore, we rebranded this concept as *Mental Availability*.[1]

The battle for brand retrieval

Retrieval from memory is a competitive process, with linked brands all vying for their place in the sun; that is, 'working memory'.[2] Much of marketing activity is about trying to nudge the odds of category buyer retrieval to be in a specific brand's favour, in the face of competitive activity and natural decay of memory. Therefore, building Mental Availability is to increase the chance a brand will be retrieved by any category buyer in any category buying situation.

The chance of retrieval depends on the link of the brand to cues used to access memory in buying contexts. Life (and segmentation models) would be simpler if everyone only interacted with a category for one reason, but as we saw in Chapter 4, rarely is this the case. If I only bought coffee to

---

1   With all rebranding, success is mixed. This highlights the importance of getting the name right first and not choosing a brand name with a meaning you might want to move on from in the future.
2   Remember from Chapters 2 and 3 that it is the part of memory where we 'work' with thoughts, but it has limited capacity so not every possible linked concept makes it into working memory.

wake me up in the morning or only bought pasta *when I want something a bit healthier*, I could easily be put in the appropriate box. But I also buy coffee to have *when friends come over*, or even when I am *cutting back on caffeine* and I reach for a brand with a good decaf option. And my pasta buying also includes situations when *I need something quick* or *craving some comfort food*. This means that classifying me into a specific segment based on my usage of the category over a short time frame does not accurately represent the full range of me as a category buyer.

A brand improves its chance retrieval when it covers as many bases (retrieval cues) as possible for as many people as possible. Therefore, Mental Availability is about building the brand's *breadth of links* across potential retrieval cues in a category. The more cues a brand is salient for, for more people, the more chance it will be evoked as an option in any buying situation.

Mental Availability management is not just about growth; it is also necessary for maintenance of share. Remember the natural state of memory is to decay. Doing nothing will lead to a decline in Mental Availability (see the consequences of this when brands go dark in Hartnett et al. 2021).

Category Entry Points (CEPs)

A 'category buyer' label is often treated like a permanently active status. However, this is not the case. Category buyers' category memories remain dormant until called into action. CEPs represent the thoughts that underpin a buyer's transition from being a person, going about their lives, to becoming a category buyer, and therefore a potential brand buyer. These thoughts activate a category buyer's memory and therefore influence which of the many known brands are the 'fortunate' ones that will be salient at that specific time.

Remember the brand is not the package: it is the Uber driver that delivers the package. I have a Lindt chocolate because *I want to treat myself*, not because I specifically want to consume Lindt. But I know that Lindt will feel like a treat, as will Godiva, and even a local brand, Haigh's.

A CEP is born ...

CEPs are pre-brand. Formed before people think about brands, CEPs come from the lives people lead, and the internal and external influences on thoughts about buying and using the category. If a thought leads to a successful outcome from buying, it can get saved in memory to be re-used to make a future buying experience a little easier. This 'memory saving' process often happens without conscious thought.

It is important to distinguish the CEPs we research from the real retrieval cues people use. On one occasion when I ordered delivery for dinner, the following thoughts shaped my options:

- I'm not feeling great (just had a flu shot).
- It's cold outside.
- My niece Gabby is visiting.
- I'm really hungry.

So, after factoring all four of those influences, several options came to mind and together Gabby and I chose from that list.

If I was researching CEPs for the food delivery category, I would not survey 'when you are not feeling great, it's cold outside, you are really hungry, and your niece is visiting' as a single CEP. Even I am unlikely to come across that combination again. However, we can break that experience down into the component parts that were influential in retrieval:

- *How I was feeling*: not feeling great, particularly hungry.
- *When it happened*: when it's cold/in winter.
- *Who I was with*: a teenage family member.

Now I will undoubtedly feel poorly and hungry, face cold weather and get takeaway with my niece at some time in the future. Therefore, each individual component is likely to influence further purchases too, either on their own or part of another combination.

Other people can also experience cold weather, eat with teenage family members, feel ill and get particularly hungry on occasion, so these components can have widespread relevance to quick service food category buyers.

How do CEPs differ from other attributes?

'Attribute' is the broad umbrella term for all qualities that could be linked to a brand in buyer memory. All CEPs are attributes, but not all attributes are CEPs. A CEP has the following characteristics:

- *Originates from category buyers* – It is sourced from category buyer lives, pre-brand.
- *Operates independently of brands* – For example, 'trust' is a brand-dependent attribute that makes little sense without the entity (brand) to trust, so this is not a typical CEP. In contrast, 'to give kids a drink' is a concept that is independent of any brands, as someone with children will need to give those children a drink even if Tropicana (orange juice), or any other beverage brand, did not exist.
- *Influences the retrieval of options to buy* – Buyers use different CEPs to create a specific sub-set that is more useful than the whole set of brands someone might be aware of in the category. For example, a list of places to catch up with a friend in the morning can differ from the list of places to catch up with that same friend in the evening. However, the list of places to catch up with a friend at 9am is unlikely to differ much, if at all, from the list of places to catch up with that same friend at 10am.

Introducing the Ws

The Ws framework gives a thematic structure to the CEPs within a category. We adapt the 5 Ws from philosophy to category buying contexts: *Why, When, Where, While, with/for Whom, with What and hoW feeling* (Romaniuk 2022). Table 5.1 describes each W and gives examples for the social media category, collected from a sample of social media users in the United States.

Table 5.1: The Ws and examples from the social media category

Why – the benefits the category satisfies

To ask or answer questions
When I want to be up to date/part of the latest conversations

When – timing aspects of category interaction, such as time of day, week, year, or the speed of the interaction (quick, slow)

Good to use in the evening before bed
When I want a quick response

Where – location for category interaction, usually relating to a physical or digital place

When on the go/away from your home
To use while at work

While – influential activities that occur prior, during or after category interaction

Something to fill in a quick break
Something to do while watching TV

with/for Whom – other people that impact the actual or desired category interaction

Connect and keep up to date with people I rarely see face to face
Interacting with someone you are interested in romantically
To connect with someone famous

with/for What – accompaniments from other categories

When I want to keep up with news/current events
To send a birthday/celebration/congratulations/thank you message
When I have a photo or video I want to share

hoW feeling – emotions before, during or after category interaction

To cheer someone up/make them smile
Good to relieve boredom
To share excitement about something that has happened (such as changes to family or work achievements)

The Ws provide a structure for working with CEPs, but you do not need to find an equal number of CEPs in every W. For example, the category of home furniture could have more CEPs in the *hoW feeling* category, as it is a category often bought for fun, fashion, self-expression or just for a change; while a category like tomatoes could have more *with What* CEPs, because tomatoes are often used as an ingredient in different dishes and the other ingredients can impact the type of tomatoes that are useful. For some categories, certain Ws are not needed; for example, we failed to find any 'where' CEPs in the toothpaste category beyond the bathroom.

How to identify CEPs

The challenge with identifying CEPs is that they are usually transient thoughts category buyers have on the way to somewhere else. To draw an analogy with transport, when we visit a place often, we develop known routes that are the easiest way for us to get there. These well-travelled routes require very little conscious effort when driving. Similarly, a well-travelled mental path requires very little conscious effort from memory.

CEPs can be thought of as 'mental pathways', and for most buying situations, most of the time, these pathways are known, so we don't pay a great deal of attention to how we get to our destination (brand choice), we just get there.

When we take new paths, we find them easier to remember afterwards because they require much more cognitive effort. A new destination means we probably plotted out a route on Google Maps and paid attention during the drive to make sure we did not miss the turns; perhaps we even got lost and had to ask someone for directions. It is an unusual situation and therefore more memorable.

For research, failure to appropriately structure questions to identify all CEPs risks only getting the unusual/'have to think about it' routes. However, it is the well-travelled routes, the ordinary 'commutes-to-work' and 'visiting your family', where category buyers spend most of their time (and money). A good CEP research method needs to uncover memories for the ordinary as well as the unusual.

The pros and cons of four approaches you can use to identify CEPs are:

1 internal 'expert' panel
2 secondary research
3 online data mining
4 primary research with category buyers.

1 Internal 'expert' panel

Marketers with category expertise can be a source of potential CEPs. However, for this avenue to work, these people need both CEP and category expertise. In my experience, when the first-time marketers provide thoughts on potential CEPs, the results are messy and mainly irrelevant.

Many of the ideas are not CEPs but draw on attribute fads at the time. The value of this process is its ability to uncover key misunderstandings around CEPs, which can then be addressed in training. Over time, as CEP expertise builds, internal experts can get better at spotting potential CEPs.

However, even an expert-generated CEP list can have blind spots that limit the comprehensiveness of the list. For example, the very common reasons people interact with the category are, perhaps ironically, common blind spots for marketers—that people buy shampoo *so their hair feels clean*, they eat eggs *for breakfast* and get insurance to *feel secure about their family's future*[3]. These fundamental category needs are relevant for many category buyers, so are important to consider when prioritising CEPs. CEP lists should not ignore the present in favour of chasing future trends.

For those in a smaller organisation and/or those whose customers are difficult to research, such as in the B2B sector, this might be the only avenue available. Therefore, using the Ws will help you generate a wider range of CEPs than using no framework at all. It might not be perfect, but it should be a better list of CEPs (for more on CEP generation in B2B see also Romaniuk 2022).

2 Secondary research

CEPs come from buyers' lives and so can be unearthed in any research that captures how buyers interact with the category. CEPs are buried in smaller, in-depth ethnographic studies and in large scale usage and attitude or segmentation studies. Reviewing past research through a CEP lens can identify potential CEPs and get additional value from past research investments. However, watch out for the following two limitations:

1 *Misinterpretation* – When research is collected and written up for one purpose, this can introduce biases, in line with the research objective. For example, if the research was undertaken because of a concern about a specific competitor, then the areas this competitor dominates

---

3   There does need to be care taken to avoid just restating the category name as a CEP. For example, if talking about body moisturisers then 'to moisturise the body' is a restatement of the category name, but *to get soft skin*, which is an outcome of using moisturiser, is a CEP. Similarly, 'to shampoo your hair' would be a restatement of the category name; however, *to get hair clean* is an outcome of using a shampoo and so is a CEP. A simple test is if it would be a Brand Awareness prompt, it is not a CEP.

might get extra scrutiny. This bias can affect CEPs coverage and presentation. Sample recruitment and types of questions might also be unduly influenced by the initial research purpose. For example, the sample might have not interviewed category buyers aged over 40 years because the focus was on understanding Generation Z. Therefore, the voices of older category buyers would not be represented in the CEPs generated from this data.

2   *Lack of comprehensiveness* – As you are using repurposed research, you have no way of knowing if all the CEPs are covered. Mapping the CEPs generated against the Ws helps identify any major gaps, but cannot necessarily provide you with the CEPs to fill these gaps.

These risks can also be minimised by a 'wisdom of research crowds' approach (Surowiecki 2004) to draw from a wide range of secondary research, conducted by different researchers using different research methods. Each piece of research has strengths that can compensate for limitations/gaps in others. The combined body of research may overcome the biases in any one specific study.

3 Online data mining

Online data is plentiful. With advances in artificial intelligence and machine learning to aid in analysis, there is the potential for companies to make more use of large volumes of text scrapped from online interactions. Does mining search term lists or social media content give insights to CEPs? The answer is *a bit*, and the size of that *bit* will vary by category.

Now before delving too much into this, I appreciate there are issues with bots, biases in algorithms as well as the processing capability you need to piece together a cohesive list from many fragmented, disparate pieces of information. These are really important issues that hold back the value of online data. But here I want to focus on the best-case scenario; that is, we are dealing with real comments about the category from real people, and we highlight the challenges using this data even if the bots and biases have been addressed.

Online data scrapping relies on revealed statements, and for a category this will depend on the need to search for information or the desire to share information. Search and/or sharing play a greater role in some categories; however, even in those categories we are not just mindlessly acting—we have thoughts before we type and those thoughts influence what we do or do not type.

For example (buckle up, this is a long one!): I might type 'Greek islands' into my search engine of choice, and from that you can discern that I am thinking about going to a Greek island. If you knew my travel history, you would see I went to Athens a few years ago, and if you had access to my Facebook account or listened into my conversations with my friends, you would be able to hear about how much I loved it and the reasons why. But even then, you would not know why I am looking up the islands rather than Athens.

You also would not know that I am also thinking about Sicily, because as I have been there before I have no need to search further at this stage. Nor will you realise that Spain is an option, but I am unsure on that because I have already planned a trip to Spain and not sure I will want to return so soon, or that Portugal is on my mind because I saw that there are more flights to the Azores and I have been curious to go since I heard a podcast from Conde Naste a few years ago.

But even if you collected all those pieces and attributed them to me, it will be very difficult to discern that the thread that ties all these together is the thought 'somewhere fun to escape the Australian winter in August'.[4]

The limitations of the best online search/data mining approaches are that the responses are biased to:

- *the unknown* – we look for information on what we do not know; we rarely recheck what we do know
- *the unusual* – which stimulates the need to search or ask others—if you can get the answer from your memory, you do not put the question in a search engine
- *the shareable* – which highlights experiences that are unusual or worth sharing—yes, I might share the new finger lime[5] trees I bought, but I am not posting about my toothpaste or toilet cleaner purchases.

---

4   For curiosity I did Google the CEP 'somewhere to escape the Australian winter in August' and the first page of search was all locations in Australia and stories about places to visit in Australia.

5   This is an Australian native lime tree that has 'caviar' like pulp that is particularly good garnish for a gin and tonic.

Even categories that feature heavily online are still prone to these biases. Therefore, online data mining can be an input, but should not be the only source consulted. There is more on the use of online data in Chapter 13, The Rise of the Machines?

4 Primary research with category buyers

We can also extract CEPs directly from category buyers if we ask the right questions. CEPs are not deep super-secret beliefs only revealed via complex probing questions. Remember they are more like familiar roads—we know when we are on them, but we are more interested in the destination rather than the scenery on the way. Therefore, the research challenge is to get people to step back and articulate the characteristics of *all* the roads they travel down, from the frequent to the rare, when they buy from the category.

We also need to consider the following:

- *Individuals are rarely unidimensional* – If you ask a person about only one experience it is easy to think that is the limit of their experience. Over time, most people come into a category across a wide range of contexts, not just one (remember Table 3.1 where category buyers experienced on average 6.4 CEPs). This means we need people's broader experiences, not just their last experience.

- *Buying and using both matter* – The buyer is the key person for research purposes, as they are the ones engaging in the behaviour of interest (buying, viewing, donating – depending on the category). However, the questions to generate CEPs span both buying and usage experience as buyers can bring thoughts about past or intended category usage to the buying situation.

- *Other people matter, but only if their opinions are salient to the buyer* – In addition to their own perspective, buyers can have memories of other people's past experiences or anticipate other people's future needs. If salient at the time of buying, these memories can shape the thoughts a category buyer has about which are suitable brands.

Here are some general questionnaire design principles to remember:

- Utilise knowledge about how human memory works. For example, there is a risk that the most recent buying/using events will unduly influence responses, so frame questions to ask about more than one category experience.

- Ask about all the Ws wherever possible—even if you are unsure of relevance to the category. This ensures you do not bias the output based on your preconceptions.
- Recognise that sometimes people have nothing to say and make that a perfectly acceptable response. This stops category buyers making up an answer to be 'helpful'.
- Keep questions focused on CEP generation—it is easy to veer off into other areas such as shopping experience or media exposure. When designing the questionnaire continually ask yourself, how does this question help me get CEPs?
- Allow buyers to answer in their own words, rather than supplying response lists. Pre-coded responses are more efficient but less effective to identify CEPs.
- Avoid directly asking people what is important to them from the category. This just gets mainly obvious rational answers (price, quality, performance) rather than useful ones.

Sample size and composition

At the Ehrenberg-Bass Institute, a CEP-identification stage for a normal consumer category typically involves around 60 category buyers. This sample size can be reduced in narrowly defined categories or where the sample is hard to recruit. Sample variety is crucial, so ensure the sample is of sufficient size that different types of category buyers are included and use quotas to boost low-incidence groups.

Help, I have too many CEPs ...

If your CEP identification research is successful, you might be suddenly swimming in a sea of 40 or so CEPs and need to reduce that list prior to any quantitative analysis. Here are two 'whittling down' approaches you can use:

1 *Sort the list into Ws to look for duplication/consolidation opportunities*
   Organising the long list of CEPs into Ws helps you see duplications. It can also reveal opportunities to combine CEPs under a greater theme. For example, in chocolate you might combine *gift for grandmother* and *gift for grandfather* into one category of *gift for grandparents*.

This is about combining two similar CEPs under a single umbrella, not creating a patchwork CEP by combining two different ideas. For instance, *a treat for kids* and for *a kid's birthday party* can be combined into *to give kids for a special event, such as a birthday party* as the evoked sets for both are likely to have a high overlap. However, it is not useful to combine *a treat for kids* and *something healthier for kids* into *a healthy treat for kids*, as options evoked *for a treat* and options evoked for *something healthier* are likely to be different. By combining the two CEPs you only get a small number of brands that match both and miss the brands that match only one. The combined CEP narrows your ability to collect brand linkages.

2 *Assess if a low-incidence CEP is pre-determined/beyond your influence*

Commonly encountered CEPs are more useful than rarely encountered CEPs. Sometimes it is possible to predict the likely incidence and cull those that are obviously low incidence now, and this low incidence is unlikely to change. For example, anything specifically around births, deaths and weddings will rarely occur.

This does not mean the CEP is unimportant overall; it might be a very profitable small part of a wider category. However, for brand tracking purposes, these CEPs can be put to the side as you know that these are never going to be widespread opportunities. You can use more specialist event triggers such as online search to signal someone has activated this CEP.

The aim is to get a manageable list of CEPs to explore further in the quest to prioritise strategic opportunities for your brand/portfolio (for more on the prioritisation process, see Romaniuk 2022).

Chapter summary

CEPs are the building blocks of Mental Availability. Building more CEPs across more category buyers to create wider, fresher networks increases the brand's chance of being bought in buying situations.

The Ws framework helps create a comprehensive list, as well as identify opportunities to reduce a long list by highlighting similar CEPs that can be removed or combined.

There are four ways to identify CEPs in a category, but best practice is to directly survey category buyers, with questions that consider the heterogeneity of a buyer's experience with the category, how memory works and make no assumptions about which Ws are more or less important in the category. Let the category buyer responses inform your thinking rather than the other way around.

If category buyer surveys are not feasible due to sample accessibility or cost constraints, then use one or (preferably) more of the other approaches and draw on the Ws framework to help overcome any blind spots that may lead to the omission of some CEP types.

The next chapter will go into more detail about Mental Availability measurement and metrics.

6

Mental Availability: Measurement and Metrics

JENNI ROMANIUK

Category Entry Points (CEPs) are the backbone of brand retrieval and form the foundation of Mental Availability. In this chapter we convert CEP-brand linkages into a measure of Mental Availability. We cover key Mental Availability metrics and the contextual factors that help interpret a brand's results, which includes painting a picture of what normal metrics look like and sharing current knowledge about deviations from these normal patterns.

The final section also highlights the limitations of some other proposed measures of Mental Availability, particularly those that rely on Top-of-Mind (TOM) measurement.

Mental Availability metrics

The three dimensions of a brand's Mental Availability are:

1 how many category buyers have a chance of retrieving the brand

2 across the categories main buying contexts

3 relative to mental competitors,[1] who are also vying for retrieval from category buyer memory.

These three dimensions can be captured in a Mental Market Share (MMS) measure (Romaniuk 2013). MMS is the share of the brand's CEP linkages relative to a representative set of competitors, across a representative set of CEPs, among a representative sample of category buyers. This relies on the right set up of the whole category buyer memory (CBM) tracker:

- Representativeness in competitors comes from having a properly constructed, unbiased brand list (see Chapter 4).
- Representativeness in CEPs comes from using the Ws framework to make sure no major types of CEPs or commonly used CEPs are omitted. Benchmarking the incidence of CEPs allows you to identify the commonly encountered CEPs, to ensure they are included (see Chapter 5). Even if it is not a priority for your brand, any commonly encountered CEP still needs to be included in the Mental Availability measure.
- Representativeness in category buyers comes from having category screeners set up correctly (see Chapter 9).

The *design for the category* lens helps you avoid biases in measurement; the analysis for the buyer allows you to create more sensitive measures and highlight changes in key growth audiences; and reporting for the brand gives you the context to better interpret the brand's results.

MMS has three underlying metrics: Mental Penetration (MPen), Network Size (NS) and Share of Mind (SOM). These metrics capture separate dimensions of MMS to help you diagnose the source of success or concerns. The next section explains this suite of Mental Availability metrics, shows how to use each metric and indicates what to expect from the results.

Mental Market Share

MMS is the size of the brand in its mental universe of CEPs and competitive offerings. The measure is relative to other brands, which means when all brands rise, the relative scores stay the same. This helps

---

1 We use 'mental competitors' because this includes brands owned by the same company that are not technically competitors, but still compete for retrieval in memory.

control for overall category influences that lift all brands but advantage none, such as seasonality which can affect buying and advertising spend. A disadvantage of this approach is that you need to have a very well-constructed, forward-looking, unbiased brand list. It is possible to handle changes in the brand list over time with interim recalculations, but this is ideally an infrequent task. MMS is a brand's CEP linkages as a share of all the CEP linkages across all brands and category buyers.

MMS = n brand-CEP linkages/Total CEP linkages across all brands

Table 6.1 shows an example taken from a data collection involving 808 respondents for a single category across 14 brands and 15 CEPs. Brand 1 received 7151 linkages from the 808 category buyers, which equates to an MMS of 24.7% of the total 28,914 linkages for all brands across all CEPs. Brand 14 received 479 linkages across that same 808 category buyers and 15 CEPs, which equates to an MMS of 1.7% of the total 28,914 linkages for all 14 brands across all 15 CEPs.

Table 6.1: MMS calculation example

	Total *n* links across all CEPs	MMS
Brand 1	7,151	24.7
Brand 2	3,823	13.2
Brand 3	2,963	10.2
Brand 4	2,825	9.8
Brand 5	2,550	8.8
Brand 6	2,124	7.3
Brand 7	1,509	5.2
Brand 8	1,166	4.0
Brand 9	1,107	3.8
Brand 10	980	3.4
Brand 11	894	3.1
Brand 12	729	2.5
Brand 13	614	2.1
Brand 14	479	1.7
Total	28,914	100.0

Is my brand's MMS normal?

A good correlation with sales share is the price of entry for any useful brand health metric. When developing an MMS measure, modelling the relationship against Sales Market Share (SMS) can provide a check that the mix of CEPs and brands is going to work.[2] It is normal for MMS to have a relatively high correlation with SMS. Normal correlation coefficients are between 75% and 95%. A scatter plot will reveal this positive, linear-like relationship between MMS and SMS.

Figure 6.1 shows the example from Table 6.1 plotted against SMS. We can see a high positive correlation (94%), which shows most brands have a normal MMS. This is a very typical chart, with most brands in line and a few brands with specific deviations.

Figure 6.1: Plotting the relationship between MMS and SMS

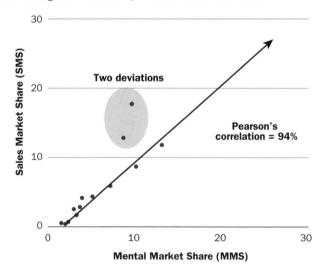

What do brand deviations in MMS mean?

First, let us remember normal (close to the line) is the best result for any brand. If a brand's MMS does *not* deviate from SMS, that brand is on a

---

2   This is an alternative to the more complicated fitting the NBD-Dirichlet, as per Romaniuk (2013).

normal path to growth. Treat deviations as red flags that identify potential problems to solve to get the brand back on the right track to grow.

But do not be surprised if you see some occasional brand-specific deviations. There are two types of deviations between MMS and SMS:

1 *MMS is higher than SMS* – This is not the time to celebrate, as while this means that a brand is 'over-performing' in Mental Availability, a common source of this deviation is a problem with Physical Availability. Something in the 'find and buy' process prevents Mental Availability translating into sales. Examples of causes include a distribution shortfall or a major gap in the brand's product range. These Physical Availability shortfalls will need to be fixed before the brand can really capitalise on Mental Availability investments (see Chapter 14 for more on Physical Availability).

2 *MMS is lower than SMS* – Mental Availability is underperforming, which suggests Physical Availability is doing most of the 'heavy lifting' to gain the brand's sales. This deviation should be taken as an indicator to review the extent or quality of the brand's Mental Availability building activities as either:

   (a) the brand is not engaging in Mental Availability building communications activities (e.g., Private Labels); or

   (b) the brand's communications are underperforming due to poor reach, inadequate branding and/or unclear messaging.

If your brand deviates from the normal relationship (e.g., is one of the brands highlighted in Figure 6.1) take remedial action if possible. If the source of the deviation cannot be fixed soon (e.g., you have a gap in your product range that you do not have the technical capability to fill), then you need to temper your growth expectations for that brand.

Evidence in support of an MMS measure

The principle behind this Mental Availability measure is that it is better for the brand to have linkages to a wider network of potential retrieval cues in category buyer memory, than to focus on only one or two specific retrieval cues. This does not mean all CEPs are equal: some are more commonly encountered, while some have less mental competition. It does mean the strategy to build the brand's links to CEPs involves spreading efforts over multiple CEPs, over time, rather than focusing efforts into trying to own one CEP (or any attribute) in line with a classic positioning/differentiation strategy (e.g., Levitt 1980, Ries and Trout 1981, Aaker and Shansby 1982).

There is no single silver bullet study that says Mental Availability is the most important CBM measure for a brand. And if there were a claim of one, I would encourage you to be sceptical as good marketing science is not based on a single study. Instead, there is a body of evidence from various categories, approaches and researchers that is slowly building up. Currently this evidence spans:

- tests between individual buyers, the size of their memory networks, and various behaviour outcomes such as future choice and future loyalty/defection
- tests of Mental Availability against other theories such as positioning or attitudes
- comparisons of brand memories held for big brands when compared to smaller brands.

Here is a range of evidence in testing areas,[3] much of which has been academically peer-reviewed and published:

- The positive relationship between the breadth of buyer's brand memory networks and actual future brand buying behaviour collected via follow-up interviews (Romaniuk 2000, Romaniuk 2003, Winchester et al. 2008).
- The positive relationship between the breadth of buyer's brand memory networks and future loyalty/lower defection in subscription markets such as banking or insurance (Romaniuk and Sharp 2003a, Romaniuk and Sharp 2003b, Trembath et al. 2011, Romaniuk 2022).
- The positive relationship between the breadth of buyer's brand memory networks and brand choice in an experimental context (Ngo et al. 2021, Stocchi et al. 2021).
- Evidence that Mental Availability is a stronger predictor of future buying intent than brand attitude in the tourism category (attitude test) (Trembath et al. 2011).
- Evidence that the total number of attribute links a buyer holds about a brand has a stronger relationship with future behaviour than any

---

3   Note due to the date of publication some of these papers refer to brand salience, but
     measurement is in line with Mental Availability as discussed in this book.

links to individual attributes (positioning test) (Romaniuk 2001, Romaniuk and Sharp 2003b).

- Bigger brands have links to more CEPs than smaller brands, therefore so a wider network is a necessary condition of big brands (Page et al. 2023, Romaniuk 2021a).

At brand level, testing has been limited because of lack of quality data over time. Indeed, it was a desire to improve the opportunities for testing that spurred my work in CEP and Mental Availability measurement. Here are two brand level examples showing the link between changes in behaviour and change in MMS from the social media category, drawing on data collected from social media users in the United States by the Ehrenberg–Bass Institute from 2019 to 2021. Figure 6.2 shows TikTok, a growing brand, has MMS trends that mirror Share of Site Visitation trends.

Figure 6.2: TikTok change in MMS over time

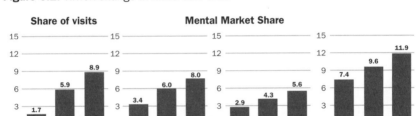

Figure 6.3 shows the metrics for WhatsApp, which has had a more turbulent ride. Its MMS metrics also mirror this rise and decline pattern, but we can see how the MMS of weekly visitors are less responsive to the growth stage than lighter/non-visitors.

Figure 6.3: WhatsApp change in MMS over time

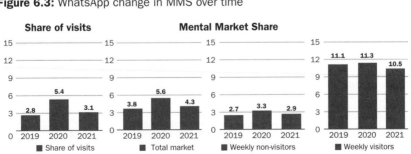

Mental penetration

MPen measurement identifies whether the brand is available in memory for *any* potential retrieval cue (Romaniuk 2013). The key differences between MPen and prompted Brand Awareness are:

- MPen goes beyond the category label as unlike traditional Brand Awareness measures, which focus on the brand's link to the category cue, MPen uses CEPs to test for possible retrieval
- MPen gives category buyers multiple opportunities to signal the brand is present in memory, which means a more comprehensive mapping of memory to check for possible brand retrieval.

These two characteristics give us a more comprehensive measure of the brand's presence in memory in the context of category buying. Prompted Brand Awareness provides a quick way of assessing a brand's presence in memory, particularly when brands are new to a category. However, once a brand has some longevity in the market, it is useful to switch to an MPen measure to assess the growth of its presence across category buyers. MPen is the proportion of category buyers who link the brand to at least one CEP.

MPen = n category buyers linking at least one CEP to the brand/Total sample size

A brand with MPen has a useful presence in that buyer's memory. This presence does not guarantee retrieval, but it is a starting point. In contrast, a brand without MPen will need to rely on something other than buyer memory to have any chance of being noticed in the buying moment. It is not 100% certain a non-MPen brand will not be bought, as sometimes interventions, such an end-of-aisle display, can attract our attention in the buying moment. However, the lack of presence in memory makes buying a more difficult outcome to achieve. Sales environment interventions to attract attention are usually costly and only temporary (see the section on rented prominence in Chapter 14).

MPen is most useful among non-buyers of brands, as this is where their potential to become future buyers will be first detected. More category buyers with the brand linked to at least one CEP widens the brand's potential buyer base.

The usefulness of MPen for bigger brands depends on whether there is room to move. If a brand's MPen is over 80%, it is more unlikely to see any major growth; instead, growth will be more likely seen in NS. MPen is still relevant to track for bigger brands, particularly among their very light/non-buyers. It is just more relevant for smaller brands where very light/non-buyers are more plentiful.

Is my brand's MPen normal?

For any brand the MPen for brand buyers will normally be 100% (or close); therefore, we are not looking for growth in buyer MPen. It is the brand's non-buyers where MPen is likely to grow.

While MPen among buyers can reveal evidence of decay, as with prompted Brand Awareness, a decline in MPen means total erosion of the brand's trace in memory, which is very late in the memory decay process. Buyer memory decline is more likely to first manifest in other metrics such as NS or SOM.

It is normal for MPen to be correlated with Sales Penetration. This analysis can substitute for the MMS versus SMS, when sales market share figures are difficult to come by such as in high impulse/out-of-home categories, subscription categories or high sole brand loyalty services/durable categories. In the example (Figure 6.4) we can see the strong relationship between the MPen and Sales Penetration, with a correlation of 95%.

Figure 6.4: Plotting the relationship between MPen and Sales Penetration

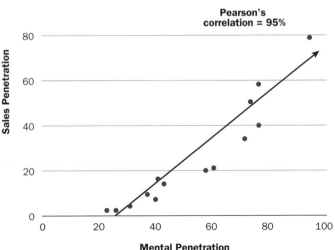

It is normal for MPen to be higher than Sales Penetration, as more people could buy than do buy in any time period. Table 6.2 shows the average scores for Sales Penetration and MPen, and brand level Pearson's correlation. MPen is 3–4 times higher than Sales Penetration, depending on the different time frames for brand penetrations and number of CEPs in each category. The average correlation of 89% shows a good relationship between the two metrics.

Table 6.2: MPen versus Sales Penetration (SPen)

Category type	Av. SPen %	Av. MPen %	Brand corr. %	Category type	Av. SPen %	Av. MPen %	Brand corr. %
HH product	37	45	99	Packaged food	13	43	96
Retail	33	74	85	Service	12	55	79
Online service	22	55	91	HH product	11	49	86
Packaged food	20	47	91	Personal care	10	52	79
Service	20	68	75	Personal care	10	43	89
Packaged food	18	47	94	Charity support	10	74	46
Service	18	60	86	HH product	10	47	90
Beverage	15	55	89	Packaged food	9	53	71
Service	15	42	92	Service	9	37	96
Packaged food	14	42	88	Service	8	60	62
				Average	16	52	89

It is also normal for MPen to be higher than prompted Brand Awareness scores due to the multi-cue aspect of MPen (see Table 6.3). It might seem odd that someone can link a brand to an attribute without being 'aware' of the brand. This is a remnant of hierarchal thinking of Brand Awareness versus Mental Availability. Prompted Brand Awareness captures the brand's links directly to the category cue, while MPen captures the brand's links to the wide range of other CEP.

Instead of seeing Brand Awareness as a precursor to Mental Availability, see the two as sitting alongside, but overlapping. Both capture different parts of the same network of memories. Someone can know a brand is a member of a category, but not have any links to CEPs, and someone else can have links to CEPs, but have the link to the category obscured due to the brand's atypical offering or a stronger presence from other brands.

Table 6.3: Examples of the difference between prompted Brand Awareness and MPen metrics

	Category 1		Category 2	
	Prompted awareness	MPen	Prompted awareness	MPen
All brands	26	43	15	50
Top 5 brands	50	57	30	61
Bottom 5 brands	10	33	10	47

What do brand deviations in MPen mean?

Brand level deviations in MPen can take two forms:

1 *MPen is higher than expected given the brand's Sales Penetration –* Similar to MMS, check for issues with Physical Availability (see Chapter 14) that might be stopping Mental Availability gains from translating into sales.

2 *MPen is lower than expected given the brand's Sales Penetration –* This usually suggests Physical Availability is effectively pulling in buyers. For example, this deviation is often seen for private label brands, which often have advantages in retail locations, but do not engage in category advertising. While this indicates Physical Availability tactics are working, you should check this is not at a disproportionate cost that harms profitability. Also look for opportunities to expand the reach of marketing activities to build a mental presence in more category buyers to protect the brand in case current Physical Availability advantages are not sustainable.

Network Size

NS captures the breadth of the brand's CEP network—are marketing activities building wider, fresher networks? It is calculated as the average number of CEPs linked to the brand, among those with MPen. NS is the average number of CEPs linked to the brand, among those with MPen.

NS = n CEP linkages for brand/n category buyers with MPen for the brand

NS is relevant to all brands and all buyers. It is a useful indicator of effective advertising messaging, as a new message should widen the brand's memory networks. Refreshing dormant memories can also create wider, fresher networks, so reintroducing a message that has been sidelined for a while could also build NS.

Is my brand's NS normal?

It is normal that when plotted against MPen, NS will show a Double Jeopardy pattern (see Figure 6.5). Bigger brands have higher MPen and higher NS, while smaller brands have lower MPen and lower NS. Table 6.4 shows this relationship across a range of different category types and countries, where the average correlation is 88%. Therefore, the normal NS for your brand, compared to other brands, typically depends on your MPen.

What do brand deviations in NS mean?

Disparities in the relationship between MPen and NS can be either of the following:

- *Lower MPen and higher NS* – This could indicate an issue with the brand's marketing activities either not reaching or not getting noticed by category buyers who don't know much about the brand. Looking for ways to minimise frequency of exposure and reallocating the spend to maximise reach can help get the brand back on a normal path if lack of reach is the problem. Reviewing brand name execution and the use of Distinctive Assets are good avenues for you to pursue if branding quality is the issue.
- *Higher MPen and lower NS* – This can indicate the brand is perceived as suiting only some of the possible CEPs in the category and is being shut out of others. If this happens first check if reflects a lack of knowledge on behalf of category buyers (e.g., we have a kid-friendly option, we just haven't told category buyers) or a genuine deficit in the brand (e.g., we don't offer any flavours kids would like).

A problem area can often be detected in other metrics, such the CEP mental disadvantages (see Chapter 7) and/or the reason for higher brand rejection rates (see Chapter 8). While a lack of knowledge issue can be addressed via marketing communications, a genuine deficit might need more extensive efforts to remedy.

Table 6.4: MPen versus NS

Category type	Country	Brand level correlation	Category type	Country	Brand level correlation
Household good	United Kingdom	97%	**B2B**	United Kingdom	88%
Service	Russia	96%	**Service**	United States	81%
Durable	Australia	96%	**Durable**	United Kingdom	79%
Service	Czech Republic	92%	**Household good**	United Kingdom	73%
Beverage	Australia	89%	**Personal care**	Germany	68%
Personal care	United States	89%	**B2B**	United States	64%
Household good	United States	89%	**Service**	Italy	58%
			Average		**83%**

Figure 6.5: The Double Jeopardy relationship between MPen and NS

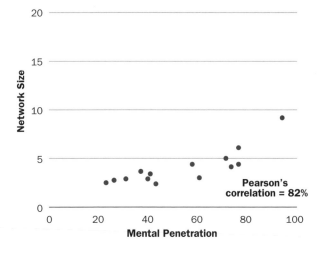

Share of Mind

SOM is like MMS, but only among those with MPen. This is the primary underlying diagnostic that directly picks up when there is a mental incursion that could have negative consequences for your brand due to an improvement in competitor activity. If a competitor makes inroads in the brain of a category buyers where your brand is present, which will be evident in a decline in SOM, the increased mental competition will lessen the chance that your brand's Mental Availability will turn into sales.

However, if a competitor impacts someone who lacks MPen for your brand, so not included in an SOM measure sample, its effect on your sales is peripheral rather than direct. Your brand was not likely to be retrieved by this category buyer, and so the competitor does not have as much impact on your brand's sales. SOM is the share of CEP links to the brand, relative to competitor links, among *only* those with MPen.

SOM = n CEP linkages for brand/n all CEP linkages for category buyers with MPen for the brand

SOM is more relevant for bigger brands and is often the first indicator of brand decline due to increased competitor activity.

Is my brand's SOM normal?

A Double Jeopardy effect, where big brands have greater MPen and higher SOM than small brands, is normal. Plotting SOM against MPen typically sees a reasonably strong relationship (see Figure 6.6). The average Pearson's correlation across the same 14 categories in Table 6.4 is 85%.

Figure 6.6: The Double Jeopardy relationship between MPen and SOM

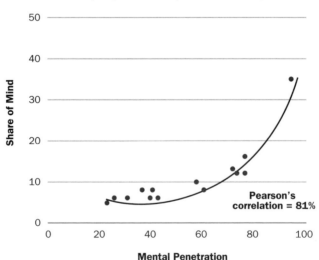

What do brand deviations in SOM mean?

It is normal for a big brand in a category to have an 'excess' of SOM, due to monopolising light buyers with only CEP linkages for one brand. For example, in Figure 6.6 the biggest brand has 35% SOM, but the nearest competitor has less than half of this at 16%[4].

We do not yet know a lot of about the individual brand level deviations in SOM against MPen or buyer behaviour as SOM deviations are not as common as in other metrics. This is an area of ongoing research as we investigate more categories and countries, and thereby get a bigger collection of deviations to explore.

Alternative measures of Mental Availability

It is possible there are multiple ways to measure the concept of Mental Availability. However, many other measures that have been proposed fall short. Most of the shortfalls in these approaches are because they assume it is important for a brand to be retrieved earlier than other brands. To date there is no evidence that this matters in real life.

Being retrieved is important and makes you more likely to be bought than not being retrieved, but there is no evidence that people will choose the first brand they retrieve from memory over a second or third brand also retrieved from memory at around the same time. Those second or third brands, once thought of, become part of the same evoked set and therefore have substantively increased their chance of being bought, as did the brand retrieved first.

The following are some alternatives to the MMS approach and their key limitations:

- *TOM awareness* – This is still being used as a Mental Availability measure, but it suffers from limitations of using a single cue, and it is too cognitively difficult for category buyers to pick up changes in memories for non/very light-brand users (as discussed in Chapters 2 and 4).

---

4   Remember that as this is a % of category buyers with MPen, the total across all brands is likely to exceed 100%, this is normal (if it adds up to 100% you have calculated SOM incorrectly).

- *TOM multi-attribute measure* – This is an extension of TOM awareness, where category buyers are asked to respond to several attributes, and the total TOM responses across the attributes are calculated. The issue with this approach, shown in Chapter 4, is that it stifles responses, particularly from very light/non-brand buyers and for small brands.
- *Time to response* – This a variation on the TOM measurement is to measure the time it takes to link a brand to an attribute. This also suffers from the untested assumption that being retrieved earlier is better than being retrieved later. The so-called 'path to purchase' is really a hiking trail with many routes that each cover very different terrain. On one occasion, only one brand will be thought of and that gets bought, but on a different occasion, three brands might be thought of and the last one retrieved gets bought, while on another occasion five brands might be thought of, but a sixth is be bought because it has stronger Physical Availability.

When we measure Mental Availability, we do not assume a single route for buyers when buying. Instead, we aim to capture the key building blocks that give the brand the best chance of being thought of by a buyer in any buying situation. This includes the:
- CEPs that can act as retrieval cues
- brand's links to these possible retrieval cues
- competitors that can impede the brand's sales.

In the survey we want to know if these links are available to category buyers and that we have improved the brand's chance of retrieval, knowing that in the real world the accessibility (order of recall) of these links will fluctuate based on many different on-the-day environmental influences.

Chapter summary

This chapter explained the fundamental qualities of Mental Availability metrics, what normal looks like, and possible explanations for deviations. The set-up of Mental Availability metrics relies on the whole CBM tracker approach to achieve a representative set of:
- category buyers through how you set up category screeners
- competitors through how you set up brand lists
- CEPs through the source of insights and the use of the Ws framework.

These three characteristics combine to create a comprehensive, unbiased Mental Availability measure and metrics. The full set of metrics are contained in Table 6.5.

Table 6.5: Summary of Mental Availability metrics and underlying calculations

	Mental Market Share (MMS)	Mental Penetration (MPen)	Network Size (NS)	Share of Mind (SOM)
Description	The brand's share of all brand-CEP links	The % of category buyers with at least one CEP link	The average number of CEPs among category buyers with MPen	The share of CEPs among category buyers with MPen
The formula	MMS = n brand-CEP linkages/ Total CEP linkages across all brand	MPen = n category buyers linking at least one CEP to the brand/Total sample size	NS = n CEP linkages for brand/n category buyers with MPen	SOM = n CEP linkages for brand/n all CEP linkages for category buyers with MPen

It also explained the limitations of measures that seek to elevate earlier brand responses in a survey, such as TOM or Time-to-Respond measures. This is not necessary and introduces additional measurement errors.

In the next chapter we will explore changes in brand attribute responses over time, both at an individual attribute level and for brand level Mental Availability metrics.

7

Brand Attributes: Analysis

JENNI ROMANIUK

This chapter focuses on the analysis of brand-attribute data collected via a free choice, pick any approach. The attribute is the focal element, and category buyers are asked which brands, if any, from a list provided, they link to each attribute. This approach is recommended because it mimics the memory retrieval process more effectively than other approaches and avoids the biases against non-buyer and small brand responses that occur without brand prompts.

The data generated by this measurement approach is often underutilised, displayed as raw percentages in bar charts or 'shudder' spider charts.[1] Therefore, this chapter is about how to take advantage of the underlying structures of this data to uncover more robust insights about the brand-attribute relationship.

This chapter will present analysis approaches that draw on or create empirically validated benchmarks for assessing the effects of marketing activities, both in the moment and over time. With more robust

---

1   I will declare a bias here; I am allergic to spider charts. I don't understand them and when I see them, I break out in hives …

benchmarks, we will be better placed to identify real changes in brand memories and the likely implications.

Marketing activity impacting brand-attribute linkages

Many organisations invest in branded marketing activities to achieve some form of behaviour reinforcement or change, such as:

- buying a brand
- viewing a program, channel or site
- attending events, including sporting, epicurean or entertainment
- supporting a charitable or not-for-profit enterprise (donation, volunteering).

A category buyer memory (CBM) tracker helps check if the conditions in buyer memory have become more conducive to these behavioural outcomes. We are going to focus on two types of effects on stored memories:

1 *Messaging effect* – If a communication piece has a well branded message, it should increase the link between the brand and the attributes that represent that message. For example, if an advertisement that the brand has low prices is successful, it should strengthen the link between the brand and *good value for money* attributes. This approach uses the individual brand-attribute linkage data (e.g., Romaniuk and Nicholls 2006).

2 *Mental Availability effect* – The marketing activity, if well branded, will also cause the brand to be retrieved, which can fan out to build wider, fresher brand memory networks. The more extensive and fresher the brand's Category Entry Point (CEP) memory network, the greater the brand's propensity to be thought of in buying situations. The approach uses Mental Availability metrics, as described in Chapter 6 (e.g., Romaniuk 2013, Vaughan et al. 2020).

Detecting messaging effects

There is great power in *knowing what to expect*. I don't mean the naive inductivist-like expectation of 'hopefully more than last wave'—we don't want to be a turkey just before Christmas here.[2] Instead, I mean an estimate of results after controlling for major inputs that influence a category buyer's response but are extraneous to the task at hand. For example, if you are wanting to test if an advertising message created more links between the brand and a specific attribute, you need to control for the influences on brand-attribute responses that are unrelated to the advertising (e.g., Romaniuk and Nicholls 2006).

There are two general factors that lead a category buyer to link a brand for a specific attribute (adapted from Romaniuk and Sharp 2000):

Past brand buying – Brand buyers are more likely to link the brand to (almost) any attribute than non-buyers (Bird et al. 1970). This is due to the depth and frequency of processing from direct experience. We see gradation even among buyers, with light buyers' response levels higher than non-buyers, but lower than heavy buyers (Hogan 2015). This increased buyer probability of response means brands with more buyers get more responses than brand with fewer buyers.

Prototypically – This is about nature of the attribute and its contribution to category membership (Rosch and Mervis 1975). Some attributes do a better job of signalling a brand is a member of a category than others. For example, in coffee *able to wake me up in the morning* is a more commonly encountered attribute than *good for when cutting down caffeine.* More prototypical attributes get attached to more brands in the category than less prototypical attributes.

The two influences of brand buying prototypically combine to reveal an underlying structural pattern to brand-attribute responses across a sample of category buyers. Table 7.1 is an example of a sub-set of attributes and brands from the social media category. When we order by row totals and column totals, you can see:

- the higher responses (cell average n=84 category buyers) come from bigger brands on higher prototypically attributes (nine cells bolded in the top left corner)

---

2   Bertrand Russell wrote this analogy as a chicken who's observations that the farmer feeds him every day leads to the conclusion that the farmer will always feed him—until he doesn't! Over time, this was changed to a turkey who starts his calculation on 15 September and for the next 99 days gets fed, which leads him to be certain that on the 100th day the farmer will again feed him, except that 100th day turns out to be Christmas.

- the lower responses (cell average n=18 category buyers) are for smaller brands on lower prototypically attributes (nine cells bolded in the bottom right corner).

Table 7.1: Example of patterns in brand-attribute data, organised by row and column totals; figures are *n* category buyers linking each social network to each attribute

	SN1	SN2	SN3	SN4	SN5	SN6	SN7	Row total
To relieve boredom	**128**	**92**	**68**	50	32	24	34	428
Good quality	**99**	**90**	**71**	58	24	31	23	396
Innovative	**76**	**66**	**62**	42	37	35	40	358
Trustworthy	60	55	38	41	21	29	14	258
Keep up with news	90	42	32	83	**18**	**16**	**11**	292
To become famous	42	96	69	40	**18**	**9**	**32**	306
Family orientated	97	47	38	15	**20**	**25**	**11**	253
Col. total	592	488	378	329	170	169	165	2291

This pattern holds across all non-negative attributes that are not simply descriptions of brand qualities. For example, if the attribute *is a small brand* or *is very different from other brands*, then responses for small brands will be heightened and responses for bigger brands will be depressed—thereby subverting the normal pattern.

At least once get the brand-attribute responses from your tracker and order them in this way to see this underlying pattern. If the pattern in Table 7.1 is not evident, then it is worthwhile investigating why not, as it suggests something might be going awry in the data collection process.

This pattern allows us, with the magic of a simple equation, to calculate an expected score for each brand on each attribute (as in Romaniuk and Sharp 2000, Romaniuk and Huang 2019).

Using two expected patterns to detect messaging effects

The message of any piece of marketing communication is in the eye of the beholder. What you wanted the advertisement to say does not matter; it is the recipient's 'take away' after experiencing the advertisement that counts. This means we must look beyond advertising content to see how the exposure to our marketing activities has changed the category buyer's brand memory networks. For example, say we want to message that the brand *now offers delivery*:

- *if* we have successfully made the brand a noticeable part of the advertisement
- *and* clearly articulated the idea of delivery being available in words and/or images,
- *then* more category buyers should link the brand to a delivery-centred attribute.

The inputs of effective messaging are a clear message *and* strong branding. The consequence of effective message building is for the brand to gain a *mental advantage* on messaged attributes, where a mental advantage is defined as the brand scoring higher than the expected score for that brand on that attribute. This 'messaging effect' is the change in mental advantages over time. Before you can assess change, you need to first benchmark the brand's attribute scores.

Tables 7.1 and 7.2 show the process for calculating mental advantages. Table 7.2 shows the expected values from the data in Table 7.1. For example, the expected value for SN1 on the attribute *to relieve boredom* is calculated in the following way:

To get the deviation from the expected scores we subtract the actual (128) from the expected (111) = 17, divide this total by the sample size (205) and multiply by 100 = ((17/205)*100) = +8 percentage point (pp) mental advantage for SN1 on *to relieve boredom*.

Table 7.2: Example of expected scores in brand-attribute data (based on Table 7.1)

	SN1	SN2	SN3	SN4	SN5	SN6	SN7
To relieve boredom	111	91	71	61	32	32	31
Good quality	102	84	65	57	29	29	29
Innovative	93	76	59	51	27	26	26
Trustworthy	67	55	43	37	19	19	19
Keep up with news	75	62	48	42	22	22	21
To become famous	79	65	50	44	23	23	22
Family orientated	65	54	42	36	19	19	18

Row total (428) * Column total (592))/Total, Total (2291) = 111

The deviations 5pp or higher are shaded to show the mental advantages for these social media brands on this set of attributes. For example, SN2 has one mental advantage in the table: *to become famous* (+15pp), while SN4 has a mental advantage for *to keep up with the news* (+20pp). SN7 has two mental advantages of *innovative* (+7pp) and *to be famous* (+5pp).

Table 7.3: Deviations from expected values to determine mental advantages and disadvantages

	SN1	SN2	SN3	SN4	SN5	SN6	SN7
To relieve boredom	8	0	−1	−6	0	−4	2
Good quality	−2	3	3	1	−3	1	−3
Innovative	−8	−5	1	−5	5	4	7
Trustworthy	−3	0	−2	2	1	5	−2
Keep up with news	7	−10	−8	20	−2	−3	−5
To become famous	−18	15	9	−2	−2	−7	5
Family orientated	15	−3	−2	−10	1	3	−4

If SN3 starts advertising it is a *good place to relieve your boredom*, and effectively builds more links between the brand at the attribute, then we would expect to see the current deviation of −1pp become positive and eventually reach +5pp or more to become a mental advantage for the brand.

How quickly a mental advantage develops depends on how well the brand's marketing activities perform on the three building blocks of reach, branding and messaging. A wide reaching, well-branded campaign with a clear, easy-to-understand message will build mental advantages more quickly than a campaign that fails in one or more of these facets.

Tracking over time

Analysis over time reveals to us if marketing activity has changed brand memories. Figure 7.1 shows an example of the results for SN1 over two waves. The attribute *family orientated* gained as a mental advantage, while *to relieve boredom* declined.

Further investigation can determine if the increase in *family orientated* is in line with messaging activities and if the decline on *to relieve boredom* is due to a new shortcoming of the brand or more effective messaging activities from competitors. The results for other attributes are largely stable[3], which is normal for most brands on most attributes.

Figure 7.1: Example of mental advantages and disadvantages tracked over time for SN1, United States

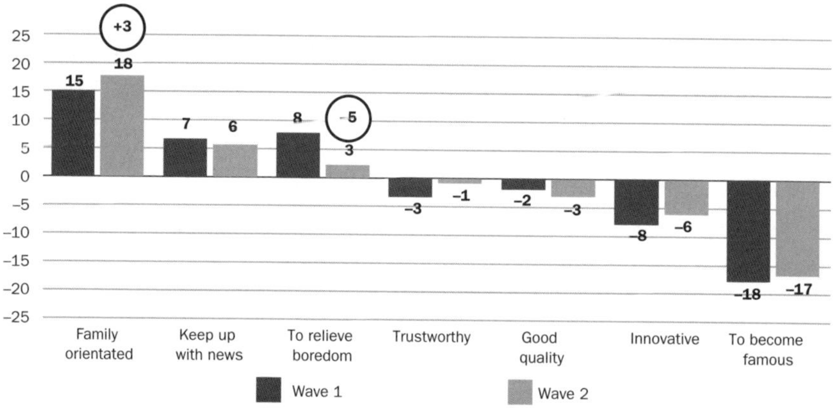

Help—I advertised a message, but no mental advantage emerged/improved

Remember that message outcomes are in the eye of the beholder, so sometimes there is simply a failure to receive anything, while other times there is a mismatch between message intent and message received. When there is no discernible messaging effect from your advertisement, potential causes are:

- *clarity failure* – the message was not clear enough to create a link to the right attribute
- *branding failure* – the branding was not strong enough to anchor the message in the right part of memory
- *competitor neutralisation* – competitors did a better job of communicating the same attribute, which often happens when

---

3   See Romaniuk and Nicholls 2006 for statistical testing if necessary. As we control for major external factors, it means it is often very easy to detect changes using a +/−3pp threshold.

advertising messages are influenced by external factors (e.g., inflation means every brand advertises its pricing/value for money)

- *reach insufficiency* – the media plan did not reach enough people to have a measurable effect.

While only one reason is sufficient to prevent a mental advantage from emerging, there might be more than one area that needs to improve for future success.

Should I try to fix mental disadvantages?

You probably noticed that the table of deviations from expected also had several negative scores. For example, SN1 scored −18pp for *to become famous*. Is this something those in the company should be worried about? The answer is *possibly yes* but *probably no*.

Only worry about mental disadvantages if they are fixable deficits in your own brand *and* the attribute is important for the brand's future. Most of the time, mental disadvantages are not of major concern because of the following reasons:

- Mental disadvantages can emerge if a competitor is particularly strong, and therefore 'drowning out' other brands. This is very hard to fix as you are going head-to-head with the same message as that of the competitor brand. Apart from the greater difficulty, this is also an opportunity cost as your brand could be messaging other, less combative attributes.
- Mental disadvantages can occur because of the functional nature of the brand and its range, and therefore are not quickly fixable (e.g., the brand does not offer a premium variant and so has a mental disadvantage for *special occasion* CEPs). In which case, ignore it until you can address the deficit.
- If it is a CEP, then that CEP with a mental disadvantage might have a low incidence. In this case, unless it is likely to accelerate in future importance, it is not worth the cost to repair the mental disadvantage, again considering the opportunity cost.

Can a brand have too much of a mental advantage?

Can you ever have too much of a good thing? Yes. Once you get to +10pp more than expected, and particularly if there are no other brands with the same mental advantage, it is time to move on to building other attribute links. Remember the long-term goal of 'wider, fresher networks'. If you keep on with the same message, then other attributes do not get their 'time in the sun'. If you stop messaging a specific quality, its mental advantage will not disappear overnight. You can put it into 'low rotation' where it is repeated every so often, but it is not the most communicated message. This is how widening the network differs from traditional 'repositioning'. When a brand repositions, it moves away from its past mental advantages as it seeks to build new ones. However, when a brand seeks to widen its memory networks, it strikes the balance between the more challenging task of building new memories, via communicating different messages to widen the CBM network, and the easier task of keeping existing mental advantages fresh.

For example, if Disney+ is extremely well-known for kid's entertainment (say it has a +25pp mental advantage), its marketing activities do not have to work as hard to constantly remind people of that linkage. The media budget is better spent reminding current and potential brand buyers of the other, non-kid's entertainment that is available. Then perhaps Disney+ might get thought of when someone is *looking for a scary movie* or *something to watch on date night*. A persistent focus on kid's entertainment is an inefficient use of resources unless that was all the brand wanted to be, or a major, big spending competitive threat emerged.

But that does not mean you should go to the other extreme and never remind category buyers about Disney+'s kid's offerings. It is important to keep that link fresh in the face of mental competition and memory decay. Remember, *low* rotation rather than *no* rotation.

CEPs versus other attributes

If you have an attribute list that includes CEPs and other attributes, it is useful to do this analysis separately for each attribute group. This reduces the impact of changes, particularly given that the list of other attributes tracked may change with company priorities.

What if the brand list changes?

Over time, there will inevitably be changes to the brand list as new brands are launched and brands get deleted. This should be a relatively rare event.

If you are constantly changing your brand list, then it is worthwhile considering if there is a flaw in your list creation process (see Chapter 4).

Removing a brand:

- Before removal, check if it had any major deviations. If there was no substantive deviation (+/–5pp), then there will be little impact on the brand's scores when you remove the brand and existing results can stand.
- If there are major deviations, then there may be some reshuffling of figures as relativities across brands on some attributes change. You will need to recalculate the mental advantages, so you have an 'apples with apples' figure to compare with the first wave without the brand. This re-analysis can be done as soon as the decision to delete the brand has occurred.

Adding a brand:

- You should review its advertising and see what messages it is sending out to identify if there are well-branded messages that are likely to result in mental advantages with tracked attributes. This will give you an indication of likely impact of the addition prior to data collection.
- Collect the data with the new brand. Then with this data create two deviation tables: (1) with only the brands comparable with last wave to assess changes over time; and (2) the full table to get the new brand benchmarks and figures for ongoing tracking.

These steps will cover you for most brand removals and additions.[4]

What if the attribute list changes?

If you need to change the attribute list, undertake the same process as for brand list changes, except with the exclusion/inclusion of the attributes that are going to/have changed.

Do I need to separate out brand buyers from brand very light/non-buyers beforehand?

As the analysis approaches controls for brand size, you do not need to do this analysis separately for buyer groups. The nature of the underlying

---

4   If you have a situation where this approach does not work, do get in touch with me and I may be able to suggest alternative options.

calculation means it is not suitable to be done on non-random samples, such as survey results from a brand's customer base, where one brand might dominate the results. For non-random samples, other approaches can be employed to calculate expected values.[5]

Detecting Mental Availability effects

The essence of Mental Availability is to aim for building wider, fresher networks among category buyers. If this is accomplished, more category buyers will think of the brand in more buying contexts.

One of the most common retrieval models of memory is called 'Spreading Activation' (e.g., Collins and Loftus 1975). This model is based on the idea that our ideas in memory are linked, and when an idea becomes a retrieval cue, this generates an 'energy' that can lead to the retrieval of any linked concepts in memory. This means the act of advertising the brand can heighten other attributes linked to the brand, including CEPs that can lift Mental Availability, separate from the messaging effect previously discussed.

The Mental Availability metrics (explained in Chapter 6) incorporate different aspects of the brand's memory network among category buyers. The primary metric is:

- *Mental Market Share (MMS)* = the share of the brand's links to CEPs relative to competitors.

  Underpinning this are the metrics:

- *Mental Penetration (MPen)* = how many category buyers have the brand present in memory
- *Network Size (NS)* = how widespread is the memory network among category buyers with MPen
- *Share of Mind (SOM)* = how competitive is the brand's memory network among category buyers with MPen.

A change in MMS, particularly among the brand's non-buyers, is the most desirable outcome. This change suggests the brand is on a positive mental trajectory among the category buyers it most needs to attract to grow. When MMS drops or rises, the underlying metrics can fill in the picture to help us understand the reasons for the change that occurred.

---

5   If you have such data, get in touch and I will help if I can.

Tracking Mental Availability over time

MMS is a relatively stable measure because it is of the competitive and CEP universe. Therefore, changes +/-0.5pp are meaningful. However, it can be sensitive to sub-category decline if this might disproportionally affect a sub-set of brands in the category. Then you will see declines for all relevant brands. For example, if your category includes brands that specialise in sparkling and still bottled water, but sparkling water is more likely to be drunk at social occasions, which were fewer during COVID lockdowns, then MMS will drop for all sparkling water brands. This is not a brand issue but a sub-category issue, and will be apparent because multiple brands with the same sub-category defining characteristic will drop. In this case, efforts to increase brand linkages to other CEPs common for the sub-category will benefit the brand.

Figure 7.2: Example of MMS changes over time for a personal care category, United States

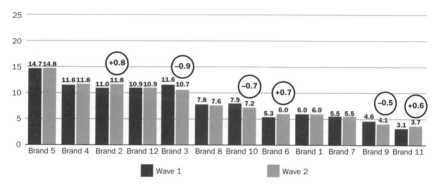

When brands grow or decline in MMS, we can 'look under the hood' to see what happened. Figures 7.3 and 7.4 are two examples from the data in Figure 7.2: a brand that grew (Brand 11, Figure 7.3) and a brand that declined (Brand 10, Figure 7.4).

In Figure 7.3, Brand 10 grew in MMS across both non-buyers and buyers, but the main metric that changed was NS. The brand has widened its CEP network but not its potential buyer base. This is not a normal growth pattern, which would be evident in a rise in MPen, particularly for non-buyers, and so should be a trigger to re-examine the branding quality to check to see it is cutting through to category buyers who know little about the brand. The marketing activity exposure Correct Branding metrics (Chapter 11) can help diagnose any branding problem here.

However, it does also indicate a successful message communication, so it would be useful to examine the mental advantages and see if there is an increase in a CEP that is linked to a specific campaign message. If it is a particularly effective campaign message, there might be the opportunity to learn why it was successful and use this knowledge to replicate the success with other messages in future campaigns.

The separate metrics therefore allow for deeper understanding of the effects of exposure to different marketing activities.

Figure 7.3: Example of deeper dive into metrics for a brand that grew in MMS

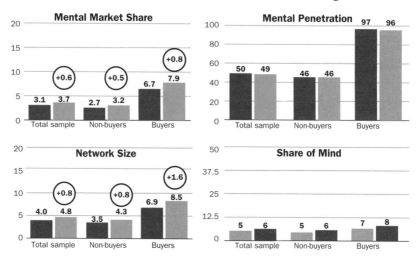

In Figure 7.4 we see the same metrics for a brand that declined in MMS (Brand 10). The underlying metrics reveal the following:

- The decline is largely among the brand's buyers; non-buyers are stable in MMS.
- Buyers declined mainly in NS; that is, CEP networks contracted— and buyers have the brand salient for fewer CEPs. This is probably due to a failure to refresh memories among existing buyers due to a decline in marketing activity spend or effectiveness.

- Non-buyers, despite stability overall, declined in MPen and increased in NS. This signals an erosion of memory that sees the brand dropping off the radar of very low Mental Availability non-buyers. This leaves the remaining buyers with Mental Availability looking slightly stronger compared to last wave. However, if non-buyers continue to be neglected by marketing activities, the excess in NS from non-buyers is also likely to decline over time, leading to MMS decline.

Both results suggest more brand level investment is needed to increase reach and refresh CEP memories to stop further decline. Separating the results out allows us to see how each of the different buyer segments are affected.

Figure 7.4: Example of underlying metrics for a brand that declined in MMS

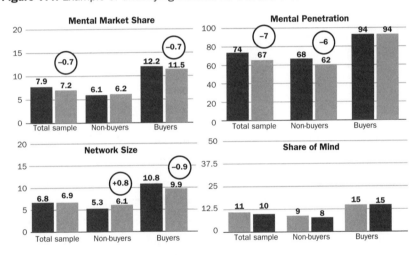

What can cause changes in MPen?

A brand's MPen should increase when the brand has reached more category buyer 'brains' through:
- improved reach in marketing communications
- improved quality of branding, so that the reach better translates into refreshed/changed brand memories
- a new message opening a new segment of buyers (e.g., advertising gluten-free options means the brand becomes relevant to gluten-free buyers).

A decline in MPen is usually due to a contraction in Effective Reach. The size of the decline relative to the decline on Effective Reach depends on the degree to which those with few CEP linkages fail to get the few brand memories they have refreshed.

What can cause changes in NS?

NS can grow:
- when there is a campaign to build a new CEP as this creates new linkages or refreshes dormant linkages
- over the life of a campaign if reach is improved such that CEP linkages are freshened among more category buyers.

  NS can decline if:
- advertising is stopped, so no brand memories are refreshed and fragile ones decay
- the execution is continued for too long and other neglected brand memories decay over time.

What can cause changes in SOM?

SOM is one of the most stable measures, so we have fewer examples of changes to explore underlying causes. It declines when a brand loses competitiveness, which can be due to the brand's failure to keep memories fresh or competitors more effectively building memories. For example, when a sub-category grows (e.g., alcohol-free beer) and there are more new entrants, the SOM of bigger brands declines, which can be a wake-up call for these big (often complacent) brands to be more competitive.

A review of competitor performance will reveal if it is due to competitors doing well. If there is no evidence of competitor effectiveness, then it is most likely a shortcoming of the brand's activities.

Chapter summary

In this chapter we covered how to use brand-attribute data in two contexts:

1 *Messaging effect* – To identify if a message has gotten through to buyers and given the brand a mental advantage in that area.

2 *Mental Availability effect* – To see if the brand is getting wider, fresher networks of CEPs, so it can be thought of by more category buyers more often.

In both cases we explored some known causes of changes over time and remedies if problems arise. These are areas of ongoing R&D in the Ehrenberg–Bass Institute.

8

Brand Attitude

JENNI ROMANIUK

Lovers of a brand will buy it; haters of a brand won't. This idea has persisted throughout marketing research since the 1950s when the concept of brand attitude entered the marketing lexicon. Building up category buyers' positive sentiment towards the brand, also known as *share of heart*, is often treated as the hallmark of marketing success.

Consumer behaviour models include positive feelings for a brand as 'higher order' effects, superior to mere *knowing* a brand, as in the famous AIDA model, with *Desire* the stage before *Action* (e.g., Fortenberry and McGoldrick 2020). Loyalty models claim buyers with both positive attitudes and behaviour are better than just buying alone (e.g., Dick and Basu 1994). However, there is only weak evidence that building strong positive category buyer sentiment is feasible, let alone necessary for brands to be bought.

In this chapter we cover how to measure brand attitude and what to expect from the results. We also discuss when capturing brand rejection is useful.

What's love got to do with it?

If Tina Turner got royalties for every time I wrote that line, she would be at least $20 richer right now. That marketers love 'love' is evident in the re-emergence of this type of concept with a new name every decade. Its current iteration is brand love, which, according to Batra and colleagues (2012), has seven dimensions of:

1 passion-driven behaviours reflecting strong desires to use it, to invest resources into it, and a history of having done so

2 self-brand integration, including a brand's ability to express consumers' actual and desired identities, its ability to connect to life's deeper meanings and provide intrinsic rewards, and frequent thoughts about it

3 positive emotional connection that is broader than just positive feelings, including a sense of positive attachment and having an intuitive feeling of 'rightness'

4 anticipated separation distress if the brand were to go away

5 long-term relationship, which includes predicting extensive future use and a long-term commitment to it

6 positive attitude valence

7 attitudes held with high certainty and confidence.

(Batra et al. 2012, p. 13)

This is a daunting list for any brand to achieve. I'm not sure even my dog Alfie loves me as much as this, and he has attachment issues!

The many measures of 'feelings towards the brand' can be grouped under the long-standing umbrella name of *brand attitude*. This umbrella covers a brand's love, hate and all the emotions in between. Trackers typically have at least one brand attitude-inspired measure, and many have several that just vary in wording. Given the various guises in which attitude measures appear, let us first step back and remember what we are trying to measure.

Another bit of history ...

The term *attitude* comes from portrait painting of the 1660s, where an attitude is the 'posture or position in a statue or painting'.[1] Cognitive psychologists later adopted this word *attitude* to represent someone's mental position on a topic, so less about someone's physical position and more about their mental disposition—do they feel positively or negatively about an idea?

---

1 https://www.etymonline.com/word/attitude

In the 1950s and 1960s, academic marketing research in the United States was heavily influenced by cognitive psychology,[2] and brand attitude was born as a category buyers' feelings towards a brand (e.g., Gardner and Levy 1955). The idea (or hope) was that if someone felt positively about a brand, then they would be motivated to act consistently with those feelings. Category buyers would buy brands they liked and not buy brands they disliked. Therefore, if we measure how buyers feel about brands, we can predict their future buying behaviour.

There are a raft of measures under the attitude umbrella, from the overall attitude measures established in the 1960s (Twedt 1967, Day 1970)[3] to more recent work on brand love and hate (Batra et al. 2012, Fetscherin 2019). The similarities across attitude measures form a useful framework to assess the many different brand attitude measurement approaches.

Components of a brand attitude measure

Brand attitude measures typically have the three components of:

1 *object* – the brand
2 *valence* – positive, negative or neutral
3 *degree* – stronger or weaker.

Table 8.1 shows how a variety of brand attitude measures incorporate these characteristics in either the question wording or response options.

---

2   In Europe, where behaviourism (think stimulus–response, Pavlov's dog and the bell) had stronger roots, attitude was not as dominant in marketing models.

3   If reading early literature that refers to 'attitude' measures, it pays to check the actual measure, as sometimes all buyer mindset measures are referred to as 'attitude measures', even when the measure is actually awareness or image (Axelrod 1968).

Table 8.1: Examples of types of brand attitude measures used in brand trackers

Measure	Valence indicators
How do you feel about the brand? With a 5, 7 or 11-point scale from 'I hate it' to 'I love it'	Positive and negative Neutral midpoint
How do you rate the brand? With a 5, 7 or 11-point scale from 'terrible' to 'perfect'	Positive and negative Neutral midpoint
How much do you agree with the statement, 'This is a brand I love'? With a 5 or 7-point Likert scale from strongly agree to strongly disagree	Positive only Unclear if neutral would be midpoint or strongly disagree
How much do you agree with the statement, 'I like this brand'? With a 5 or 7-point Likert scale from strongly agree to strongly disagree	Positive only Unclear if neutral would be midpoint or strongly disagree
How appealing is this brand to you? Very appealing Quite appealing Not very appealing Not at all appealing	Positive and negative Neutral scale point is unclear
Which brand is your favourite? With a list of brands provided, single response	Strong positive only Mild positive, neutral and negative all non-response
Which brands do you love? With a list of brands provided	Strong positive only Mild positive, neutral and negative all non-response
Which of the following best describes how you feel about each of the following brands? With a verbally anchored scale from this list: 'It's my favourite' 'It's one I prefer' 'It's one I wouldn't usually buy but would if it was on promotion or the only one available' 'It's one I would refuse to buy' 'I have no opinion on/unfamiliar with this brand'	Positive, negative and neutral

It's nice to be loved, but is it necessary?

Before we go too far down this rabbit hole, there is a large body of evidence that shows attitudes tend to follow behaviour rather than drive it (for a summary of this, see Sharp 2017). The attitude–behaviour relationship is often weak, with people stating a particular positive or negative attitude to something and then failing to behave in line with that attitude (e.g., work on environmental attitudes and behaviours such as in Wright and Klÿn

1998) or quickly behave in conflict with that attitude when faced with an opportunity to act (e.g., right back to LaPiere 1934).

One of the key reasons for the disconnect between attitudes and future behaviour change is that we rarely form an opinion of something we have not experienced. *After* someone buys a brand, assuming it served its buying purpose, positive feelings *can* be generated. This positive evaluation can then feedback to future purchases *if the attitude is remembered in the future*. If the brand has not served its purpose, then a negative attitude can be generated, and this can dissuade future purchases, *if remembered*.

Therefore, our key audience for growth, brand non-buyers, are unlikely to express an attitude; and while brand attitudes can affect buyers, this only happens if the attitude is remembered. These restrictions do not make attitudes irrelevant, but they do temper any expectations that a magic bullet indicator for future brand growth will emerge from measuring *how people feel* about brands.

Some of the misplaced assumptions about the effect of attitude on buying behaviour come from a lack of descriptive knowledge about how different levels of brand attitude are normally spread over a category buyer population. Once we understand how many category buyers typically love, hate, like a little, dislike a little, or have no feelings at all towards a brand, we are better placed to understand the role of attitude in buying or not buying.

Distributions of brand attitudes

Let us first look at the brand attitude distributions from two different attitude scales (Figure 8.1 and 8.2). The response distribution of a typical brand attitude measure skews to slightly positive. Very few category buyers have negative opinions about brands, but also few category buyers have very positive opinions. Category buyers are much more likely to be unaware or have no opinion than actively reject/hate a brand.

These patterns vary predictably with brand size, with bigger brands skewing more to positive and smaller brands skewing more to neutral. If you doubt this is normal, check this for yourself in your own category—you probably have this type of data already collected. Just make sure your measurement covers all category buyers, so you can see the full spectrum of attitudes to your brand.

Figure 8.1: Attitude distributions for a 7-point love–hate scale in a food brand, United Kingdom

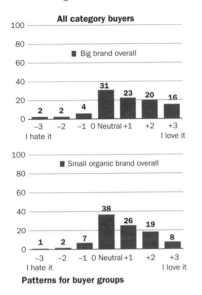

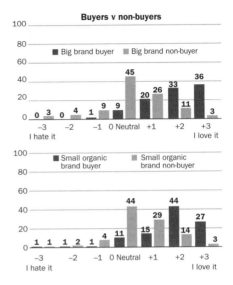

Patterns for buyer groups

Patterns for buyer groups

Underpinning this overall distribution are the different distributions for buyers and non-buyers (again see Figures 8.1 and 8.2 for examples). Brand buyer attitudes about a brand are more positive than brand non-buyer attitudes because attitudes are largely developed due to experience, and past brand buyers have more experience. Therefore, past behaviour is an important contextual lens for interpreting brand attitude results.

Brand buyers

The brand's buyer attitudes tend to peak at the slightly positive indicator, surrounded by a few buyers neutral in sentiment and a few buyers having a stronger positive attitude. This means it is important for an attitude scale to have a mild positive attitude point so brand buyers are not forced to choose between expressing strong positive attitude or nothing at all.

Brand light/non-buyers

Non-buyers of the brand tend to peak at the neutral response level (or midpoint of the scale if the neutral indicator is not explicitly labelled), with a few non-buyers expressing a negative sentiment (usually lapsed buyers), a few non-buyers slightly positive and very few non-buyers that are strongly positive. Therefore, it is important for an attitude scale to have a neutral point so that category buyers with no opinion are not forced to make one up to answer the question.

Figure 8.2: Attitude distributions for a 7-point verbally anchored scale in a personal care brand, China

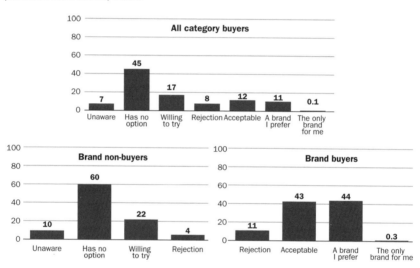

Make it OK for category buyers to not have a brand attitude

Any measure of attitude to the brand needs to capture the full range of possibilities, including having no attitude at all. The assumed pre-eminence of brand attitude can often blind us to the fact that it is possible to know something and not have any feelings towards it. For example, I know Neptune exists, but I don't have any feelings towards the planet (or the Roman god for that matter). A good attitude scale gives everyone a 'home', including those who 'got nothing' when they are asked how they feel about the brand.

Very few people use the negative part of an attitude scale, so do not waste lots of scale points capturing degrees of negative attitude.

The distribution reveals ...

Data distributions can tell us a great deal. The normal distribution for a brand's attitude across category buyers tells us that few buyers (or non-buyers) have strong negative or positive feelings about a brand. This means most buyers do not need a strong attitude to buy a brand, which also means non-buyers do not need a strong brand attitude to start buying the brand.

This immediately releases the pressure on a marketer to somehow build love for a brand from most category buyers who are ill-equipped experience or interest-wise to hold strong feelings for the brand. Hoping category buyers will convert from brand ambivalence to brand love and then suddenly buy will leave you disappointed.

It is possible to love a brand and not buy it, but that is usually only when there is a barrier to purchase (it is too expensive or not available, as in the case of many luxury goods). In this case the positive brand attitude is unable to convert into revenue for the brand, so is of questionable value to build.

Future telling but not future driving ...

The attitude distributions for larger and smaller brands give insight into what happens to brand attitude if a brand grows. Figure 8.3 shows the change in attitudes for ten brands that grew in share year-on-year. The attitudes for all category buyers show the following major changes: a decline in those unaware of the brand and an increase in those with no opinion who find it acceptable or who prefer the brand. Brand rejection and strong positive attitude scores are unchanged among these growing brands.

Figure 8.3: Change in attitude over time for ten growing brands in a personal care brand, China—differences over 1pp highlighted

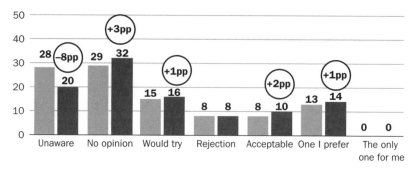

Brand rejection

Brand rejection occurs when a buyer states they dislike/would refuse to buy a known brand due to a (perceived or actual) deficit or flaw. This differs from rejection due to the brand being unknown (see Chapter 2 on Brand Awareness), where the remedy is to build prompted awareness and Mental Availability. If the brand is rejected due to a deficit or flaw, then Mental Availability building activities among those rejectors *might not* pay off in sales increases unless the flaw/deficit is addressed.

The '*might not*' is important here as attitudinal rejection does not always mean behavioural rejection. This was illustrated to me via my niece Gabby, who often loudly stated her dislike of Hungry Jacks (Australian Burger King) and refused to enter any store. At least that was her behaviour until when returning from the United States, Hungry Jacks was the only place she could get fast food for breakfast in Sydney's domestic airport terminal. She did not even blink, let alone agonise, and just headed over to make a purchase.[4]

Rejection benchmarks reveal if brand rejection is a potential problem for the brand. This is rarely the case as typically rejection scores are similarly low across all brands in the category (Romaniuk et al. 2012). However, benchmarking brand rejection, particularly among non-buyers, helps combat any marketing team assumptions that non-buyers do not

---

4   When I told her at the time that she would be my poster child for the disconnect between attitudinal and behavioural rejection, she just shrugged and ate her hash brown.

buy the brand because of negative sentiment, and you need to direct marketing effort to convert negative sentiment into positive sentiment before the brand will be bought. Rejection benchmarks typically reveal that most non-buyers have no negative sentiment towards the brand. This can be an important step forward in everyone developing a Mental Availability mindset.

However, after benchmarking, there is no need to pay any more attention unless the brand undergoes a radical change or if there is negative publicity about a brand or company. On the rare occasions where brand rejection metrics reveal a large entrenched negative sentiment towards the brand, you can work towards addressing this or, if necessary, switching resources to a brand with fewer attitudinal barriers to purchase.

Getting additional insight from the reasons for rejection

For those who state they reject the brand, having a follow-up question on the reason for rejection can be useful to identify if there is anything easily fixable that can reduce a problematic rejection rate. This data is best collected via open-ended responses rather than using pre-coded response sets, so you can understand the issue in category buyers' own language.

It may seem more efficient to pre-code the data, but that makes it too easy for someone to pick a logical response rather than articulate the proper issue. Do not be surprised if, when asked to explain, brand rejectors cannot articulate any specific reason for their position. This means that brand rejection is even less of an issue than the (usually low) scores would suggest. Typically, there are few brand rejectors and you only need to analyse this data for unusually high, changed, or new brands, or existing brands facing a predicament. Therefore, the questionnaire and analysis load are not onerous.

New launch rejection check

When a new brand or line extension is launched into the category, brand rejection questions can:
- identify any concerns about the concept that might hamper trial
- identify any negative experiences from new buyers.

Social listening tools and online reviews can get you the 'loud voices' that might have influence on others but represent only a small section of buyer experiences. Measuring the rejection level of the new launch across a representative set of category buyers can help you get a more balanced opinion. If rejection is unusually high, then the reasons for rejection might help you diagnose the issue.

How to effectively use an attitude measure

Once you have a measure that captures the full range of possible attitudes, then it is about knowing how and when to use this data. Here are some suggested steps:

1 Benchmark the distribution of category buyers' attitudes to the brand, and check it is normal for a brand of your size within the category, both overall and separately for buyers and non-buyers.

2 Create separate benchmarks for brand rejection among brand buyers and non-buyers to check if these scores are low and similar to competitors. Have this chart handy to remind everyone that most non-buyers have no rejection barriers to purchase.

   • If your brand's rejection rate is unusually high, examine the reasons for rejection to check to see if there is anything that can be addressed.

3 After this set up, you only need to measure brand attitude when:

   • *your company launches a new brand or variant* – as a check for barriers to purchase that could be addressed early and give the new launch a better chance of success

   • *competitors launch a new brand or variant* – get an initial read on the market presence and likelihood of longevity (combined with awareness and buying metrics)

   • *negative publicity about the brand* – that might reach non-buyers and cause an increase in brand rejection and reduce their chance of becoming future customers.

Having an attitude measure programmed into the questionnaire, but only reporting on it when necessary, saves resources and stops the tracker deck being filled with metrics that are not expected to change. Brand attitude is a small part of the story of brand health. It is not irrelevant, just often unimportant.

Chapter summary

One measure of brand attitude is sufficient, so the first step is to check your brand tracker for redundancies. You might be unnecessarily measuring the same 'feelings towards a brand' in different questions and therefore can remove duplicates and not lose insights.

Going forward, check your brand attitude measure:

- allows for the full spectrum of attitude responses, including no attitude/opinion
- allows you to quantify the level of brand rejection
- follows up brand rejectors with a question to capture their reason for rejection
- allows you to separate out rejection scores for brand buyers and non-buyers.

The most useful times to consult a brand rejection measure are: (a) to assess the acceptance of a new launch (yours or competitors); (b) if the brand changes substantively; or (c) there is a burst of negative publicity. Your brand rejection metrics can quantify the extent to which brand rejection is of concern and provide insights to help address any issues.

9

Category Buying Behaviour

JENNI ROMANIUK

ategory buying questions are in two areas of a brand tracker
questionnaire. The first place is at the start, to identify potential
respondents. The second place is later in the questionnaire, where more
detailed questions capture category buying frequency and sub-category
buying. These questions about the incidence and frequency of category
buying can influence the quality of the research sample, help evaluate
the brand's marketing activities and provide additional insights into
category structure.

This chapter deals with how to design these two types of category
buying questions and to make good use of the data that is collected. It
also highlights the importance of understanding category buying patterns
when designing brand health questionnaires.

Buyer, user, consumer or customer

There are two types of people we might want to recruit:

1 *The category buyer* – The person who transacts with the brand/
company in the category behaviour of interest (e.g., buying, watching,

donating). Other names for this person are the customer[1] in business-to-business contexts, subscriber in media contexts, or supporter in not-for-profit contexts. For convenience, we use 'buyer' throughout this book to cover all these labels.

2 *The category user* – The person who reaps the benefit of the act. This is often the buyer, but can be others, such as children, other members of the household, or the recipient of a gift. Other names include the customer in business-to-consumer contexts, or the viewer in media contexts.

Category buyers engage in the behaviour of most value to the brand; therefore, these are the people to recruit for a category buyer memory (CBM) tracker. Secondary audiences who use the category but don't 'buy' can be influential (e.g., pester power in kids), but the buyer is still the gatekeeper of that influence. Only remembered user preferences influence the category buyer. Surveying the category buyer gets you the best of both worlds. It allows you to capture buyers' memories of other people's opinions, as well as their own memories about the category and its brands.

Getting to know the category

Before designing a category or brand buying measurement section, it is useful to take stock on how the category is bought. Here are three areas of information that will help you get to know what *typical* buying looks like in your category, and how buying varies over category buyers. This information can be sourced from recorded panel or transaction data or collected from category buyers directly via surveys. The results help you to design a questionnaire that captures the natural heterogeneity across your category buyers' buying behaviours.

1 Category Purchase Frequency

In many categories, buyers can buy multiple times. When this can happen, it is useful to understand the frequency distribution, or how many people are at different frequency options from zero to the maximum. The number

---

1   This gets a bit confusing as sometimes 'customer' refers specifically to the brand's buyers, not category buyers. This ambiguity is why I prefer not to use the 'customer' label.

of times category buyers buy from the category in a period is referred to as Category Purchase Frequency (CPF). This distribution ranges from zero to a maximum that varies across categories and timeframes.

Mapping this distribution across a range of timeframes such as a week, month, quarter and year allows you to understand how the ratio of light and heavy buyers changes during time periods of different lengths. You can then select a sensible time frame for sample recruitment and to monitor changes to category buying metrics over tracking waves. Viewing the CPF also helps you understand the mindset of typical buyers within the category. The more people that buy the category infrequently, the harder it will be to remember the category and the brands within. Average CPFs can give a misleading view of most category buyers, due to the long tail Negative Binomial Distribution (NBD) (Ehrenberg 1959). Looking at the full distribution gives you a more realistic perspective.

In other categories, such as those with an annual subscription, the CPF is typically one for all category buyers. However, even these CPFs can vary. For example, mobile phone service subscriptions can be multi-device use, or family plans, which can count as more than one purchase. Growth in this part of the market can shape the future of the category; for example, more family plan buying could mean fewer individual accounts from new (younger) category buyers. This then affects how new buyers learn about brands in the category. Therefore, when doing a category audit, capture CPF for all categories, even those where relevance looks low.

When selecting your time frame, remember that a very short time frame will stifle your ability to see heterogeneity in category buying. For example, Figure 9.1 shows how the distribution for packaged goods changes over time periods of a month to a year, while Figure 9.2 shows the category buyers that get added if you extend the time frame from last month to in the last three months.

The screening question of *bought in the last month* excludes 20pp of people who will go on to become category buyers later in the quarter. While this 20pp includes light category buyers, the 10pp who bought once only, it also includes 5pp who went on to buy twice, and so on up to the additional 4.7pp who bought 3+ times in the quarter, just not at all in the first month (perhaps they were on holidays!).

Therefore, a longer time frame gets a wider range of category buyers than a shorter time frame. This time frame extension does not just let in more light buyers, but also some medium and heavy buyers too. There's more on selecting a time frame for sample recruitment later in the chapter.

Figure 9.1: Example of packaged goods changes in CPF distributions over different time periods

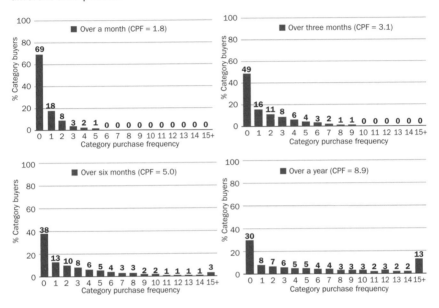

Figure 9.2: Illustrating change to the buying frequency distribution when the time frame is extended from one month to three months

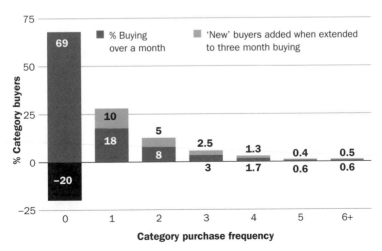

2 Repertoire size

The number of brands that category buyers buy in any time period is referred to as their *repertoire size*. This can range from one brand (solely loyal) to as many brands in the category.

To get this figure, calculate how many brands the category buyers bought in a suitable time frame such as three months (if frequently bought) or a year (if less frequently bought).

The distribution of the number of brands in category buyer's repertoire reveals the level of knowledge that your brand's buyers will have for competitor brands. If most people use only one brand in the category, most buyers will have low knowledge about competitor brands; while in categories where most people buy from multiple brands, competitor knowledge will be higher.[2] This analysis also informs whether your brand buying questions need to be in multiple or single response form.

Figure 9.3 illustrates the average repertoire sizes and underlying distributions for five different categories: three services and two packaged goods. In all categories some buy one brand only, but many buyers' repertoires comprise three or more brands. Even the banking category, with 46% sole brand loyalty, still has 30% of category buyers with three or more brands in their repertoire.

3 Shopping behaviour

Knowing how people shop the category helps understand the memorability of buying behaviour. Some categories can be bought in very different environments (e.g., from a vending machine) or for atypical purposes (e.g., gifting). Any channel or buying occasion that is likely to be forgotten due to lower prevalence or clutter from other activities at the same time should be specifically highlighted.

For example, Table 9.1 shows the varied channels for buying a type of alcoholic beverage (e.g, vodka or gin) in the United Kingdom. The wide variety of channels risks buying in less salient channels being forgotten. For example, it is easy to forget duty-free alcohol purchases with the

---

2   The amount of brand advertising for the category also impacts competitor knowledge and so should also be considered, but repertoire size matters more because buyers tend to notice advertising more for brands they buy (Vaughan et al. 2016).

Figure 9.3: Distribution of brand repertoire sizes across five categories

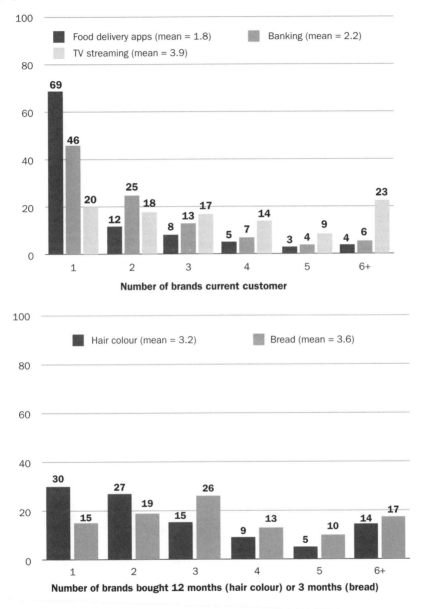

excitement of the travel that occurs at the time, or restaurant alcohol buying due to buyer memory being distracted by the fabulous food. In these situations, channel prompts in the category buying question will improve buying memory.

Table 9.1: Shopping channels for a type of alcoholic beverage

Off premise	% buying	On premise	% buying
Supermarket/hypermarket	75	Pub	49
Convenience store	36	Bar	32
Discounter	29	Restaurant	28
Online	26	Premium/Gastro pub	23
Specialist liquor store	23	Nightclub	22
Duty free	20		
Club store	15		

4 Category growth dynamics

Categories can grow via adding more buyers, getting buyers to buy more, or getting buyers to pay more (Dunn et al. 2021). If your category grows by adding buyers, then it might be useful to identify new category buyers so you can check if they are being reached with the brand's marketing activities.

If the category is in decline, it can be useful to investigate lapsed category buyers. However, this research is best conducted as a stand-alone study, as many future lapsed category buyers do not yet realise they are going to lapse. CBM surveys could find category buyers that have consciously made the decision to stop buying the category in the future, but this is only one type of lapsed category buyer. We do not notice when memory decays and we forget to buy. Other research approaches will give you more insight into possible ways to arrest category decline.

'Get to know the category' summary card

Tables 9.2 and 9.3 show two examples of 'get to know the category' cards. After it is set up, keep it visible and update the card every couple of years to see how your category changes.

These four areas are ubiquitous across different categories, which is why they are the focus of this section, but they do add important characteristics specifically relevant to your category. With a thorough overview of the category's buying behaviour, you are better placed to design good category and brand buying questions for your tracker.

Table 9.2: 'Get to know the category' summary card questions and example responses for a packaged goods category

Area	Questions	Answers (for a specific time period)	Notes
Category Purchase Frequency	How often do buyers buy the category?	Distribution of category buying frequencies ■ Over a year (CPF = 8.9) 100 / 80 / 60 / 40 / 20 / 0 30 8 7 6 5 5 4 4 3 3 3 2 3 2 2 13 0 1 2 3 4 5 6 7 8 9 10 11 12 13 14 15+	Category penetration in a year is 70%. One in four buy less than once every three months. One in five buy once a month or more often.
Brand repertoire size	How many brands do people buy from?	Distribution of brand repertoire sizes 100 / 80 / 60 / 40 / 20 / 0 14 21 22 17 12 6 4 2 1 1 1 2 3 4 5 6 7 8 9 10+	Only 14% are solely brand loyal. Most buyers buy 2–4 brands in a year. One in four buy five or more brands per year.
Shopper behaviour	How do buyers shop the category?	% using each channel 73% bought in supermarket/hypermarket 24% bought online via supermarket/hypermarket site 22% bought from a club store (e.g., Costco) 18% bought in a convenience store 3% bought from an online-only marketplace	Supermarket/hypermarket is the main channel. One in four bought the category online. One in five bought from a convenience store where impulse purchases are more likely.
Category growth dynamics	Is the category growing?	Growth level 0 – Category is mature and stable	No modifications/additions needed.

Table 9.3: 'Get to know the category' summary card questions and example responses for a software service category

Area	Questions	Answers (for a specific time period)	Notes
Category Purchase Frequency	How often do buyers buy the category?	Distribution of category buying frequencies	
		Once a year or less frequency, depending on contract length	Buying is very infrequent.
Brand repertoire size	How many brands do people buy from?	Distribution of brand repertoire sizes	
			32% are solely brand loyal. Most buyers are customers of 1–3 brands in a year.
Shopper behaviour	How do buyers shop the category?	% using each channel across brands 62% went straight to a company website 54% contacted by a sales rep 50% via online search 38% clicked on a social media post 37% clicked on an online ad 34% via contact at an event An additional 25% on average came via a third-party source (broker etc.)	Direct to company is the most common path. One in four comes from an intermediary. High proportion going straight to company website highlights the importance of building Mental Availability.
Category growth dynamics	Is the category growing?	Growth rate Category growth rate is 18%	Market is expanding, so need to identify new category buyers.

Category buying metrics

The two primary category buying metrics are category penetration and category buying weight.

Category penetration

It is hard to recover from a poor sample, which places a great deal of importance on the choice of the screening question(s). Keep *design for the category* in mind. It is not just about your brand; it is about your brand in the wider category context. You want to be able to assess threats from competitors and for the CBM tracker to work for your brand in the long term. Therefore, the sample you recruit should work for any brand in the category, whether large, medium or small, not just your brand right now.

Your screening questions need to recruit based on category buying, not category using, to ensure you are measuring memories of a sample who directly contribute to the brand's performance. In a brand tracker it is better to have someone who buys but does not use than someone who uses but does not buy.[3]

In durable and service categories, category penetration is relatively easy to measure as ownership of the category product/service with questions like: Do you have a mobile phone? Do you have a credit card? Do you subscribe to any TV streaming services? Sometimes a combination of products can be the basis for screening (e.g., having any one of ten possible business insurance products). If someone does not know if they, their household or their business has that product, then they are not the best person to complete the questionnaire.

In categories such as packaged goods, buyers have different inter-purchase intervals. This means you need to include a time frame, such as *having bought <insert category> in the past three months*, to separate buyers from very light/non-buyers (Dawes et al. 2022). The length of this time frame, whether it is one month, three months, 12 months or longer, is an important decision.

---

3   There might be other research where the user is a more appropriate sample, such as product testing.

Identify a 'Goldilocks' time frame

If the time frame is too short, your category buyer base will skew to heavier category buyers, as many light buyers have not yet had a chance to buy. For example, if you ask milk buyers about milk bought yesterday, then anyone who bought will have had only time to make one purchase, and those who make this one purchase are more likely to be heavy category buyers. If you ask over a month, there are opportunities for more purchase occasions and more chances for lighter category buyers to indicate their status through their behaviour.

However, a time frame can also be too long, and can inadvertently include lapsed category buyers. This will dilute the usefulness of the information gathered from the sample. As memory decays when not used, lapsed category buyers have lower levels of information about all brands in the category. This will depress brand level metrics.

A 'Goldilocks' time frame is long enough for category buyers to have bought multiple times if they want to, but short enough for purchases to be memorable. As such, the most useful time frame varies with CPF and memorability of the buying event. Here are some examples of common time frames and categories where they can be useful:

One week – *buying that can happen for most category buyers at least once a week, such as TV viewing, social media usage or transport decisions.*

One month – *buying that happens for most category buyers between once a week and once a month, such as buying eggs, bread or out-of-home food. This might also be relevant for broader categories such as 'any alcoholic beverages', or 'any snacks'.*

Three months – *buying that happens for most category buyers between one and three months, such as buying yoghurt, chocolate, coffee pods or specific sub-categories such as energy drinks or everyday/standard whisky.*

12 months – *buying that happen less often than once in three months for the vast majority of category buyers, such as buying skincare, toilet cleaner, champagne, deodorant or premium whisky.*

Over 12 months – *this should be reserved for bigger purchases that are more memorable events, such as holiday destinations, luggage or more expensive luxury purchases such as handbags.*

If you are unsure, experiment—ask about buying over incrementally longer time frames and compare the brand repertoire sizes (as shown in Banelis et al. 2013). You will see when the effects of lengthening the time frame on the repertoire size taper off, and further extending the time frame does not substantively expand the size of the repertoire you capture in the data.

Take steps to minimise 'telescoping'

While a time frame is essential to classify category buyers, this introduces the risk of telescoping. Telescoping is when category buyers are asked about purchases in the last three months but respond with purchases over a longer period, such as a five-month time period. The act of buying might be accurate, but the time frame is not. This leads to an over-estimation of buying for categories that are regularly, but infrequently bought, like toilet cleaner or shampoo (Ludwichowska 2013).

A bounded recall approach helps minimise telescoping (Ludwichowska 2013). This involves asking about buying in a longer 'reference' time period first, before the shorter 'target' time period. For example:

- If your target time period is *one week*, then you can use one month as your reference time period.
- If your target time period is *3 months*, then you can use 12 months as a reference time period.
- If your target time period is over *12 months*, then you can use last three years or 'ever bought' as a reference time period.

This dual questioning approach reduces over-claiming in the buying figures that respondents give for the target time frame.

Sub-category penetration

Broader categories can have sub-categories where penetration questions are helpful to calculate sub-category incidence, or to screen for respondents to get further sub-category buying questions. The sub-category time frame should preferably replicate the category time frame. If you vary the time frame for each sub-category, it will be hard to interpret sub-category buying results in the context of the wider category.

Category buying weight

Measuring buying weight lets you to classify category buyers into heavier and lighter buyers. While both heavy and light category buyers are useful in a CBM tracker, light category buyers are often omitted or ignored.

Why light category buyers are useful

A common mistake in tracker sample design is to skew the sample to heavy category buyers, either directly, through screening on buying frequency/ or amount (e.g., needing to have paid over $500 for clothing in the past three months), or indirectly, through imposing a very short buying time frame to qualify for the sample (e.g., must have bought chocolate in the last week).

Any CBM sample needs a relatively normal balance of light, medium and heavy category buyers. Light category buyers are important to include because they:

- provide a good test of the reach of your marketing efforts, because if you are reaching light category buyers, then you are reaching one of the hardest targets in the category
- include a disproportionate amount of new category buyers, who you want to reach and understand to future-proof your brand, because just to stay stable in market share, a brand needs to get a 'fair share' of new category buyers
- can be the source of future category growth as they have room to increase their purchases.

While light category buyers are important, heavy category buyers are also useful, particularly when assessing the performance of new launches. These buyers are typically the first to buy a new launch (Trinh et al. 2016) and so can provide early signals about new launch acceptability and performance.

Constructing a category buying weight measure

To construct a category buying weight measure, draw on the nature of the category and characteristics collected from the 'getting to know the category' card. In service or durable categories, if there are multiple sub-categories then you can sum across the products and use a *number of products* to measure for buying weight. If there is only one category then you can use questions about number of transactions and account value to weight buyers, where you are confident in the accuracy of the responses.

In repeat purchase categories, such as most consumer packaged goods, how many times people bought from the category (category buying frequency) is a good measure of buying weight. Our brain has an automatic frequency counting process that subconsciously keeps track of how often an event occurs. This counting happens in the background without any notice, but we can call on this tracked count if asked and give a reasonably accurate frequency score (as identified by Hasher and Zacks 1984). Someone might not be able to remember if it is exactly four or five purchases, but they would know if it was four or five, not just one purchase, and not ten purchases.

Buying frequency measures can still be prone to error if we ask people to remember over long time frames. When purchase occasions are many, buyers can take shortcuts to calculate the response and these shortcuts introduce errors (Ludwichowska 2013). As buyers differ in buying rates over the same time frame (some might only buy once, but others over ten times within the same category), the errors are more concentrated in heavier category buyer responses. Two common errors for heavier category buyers are (from Ludwichowska et al. 2017; also see Figure 9.4):

Averaging – if asked how many times the brand has been bought in the last three months a heavy buyer can think *I buy about once a week* and so give an answer of 12 times, even though in the last three months they actually bought 11 or 13 times. Evidence this is occurring in data is via 'bumps' in the frequency distribution for relevant time-period increments (e.g., seven times (days) if asking about a week, four times (weeks) if asking about a month, and 12 times (months) if asking about a year). These bumps are often accompanied by dips in the surrounding numbers, such as six and eight times (days); three or five times (weeks) and 11 and 13 times (months).

Rounding – is when people round up or down to the nearest increment of five or ten. This is apparent in frequency distribution bumps at five or ten increments and again dips in surrounding numbers. For example, eight, nine, 11, or 12 purchases are lower, if (heavy) buyers are rounded to ten.

Figure 9.4: Example of averaging and rounding errors

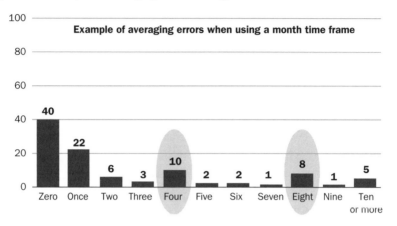

Example of averaging errors when using a month time frame

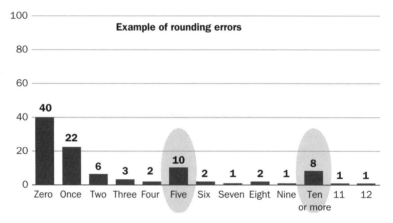

Example of rounding errors

The approach to fix these errors depends on if you need to correct at overall category level or individual buyer level.

Category level fix

If you need category level metrics to be as accurate as possible, you can take advantage of the NBD (Ehrenberg 1959). Fitting the NBD can provide estimations for each frequency group and properly identify errors (Ludwichowska et al. 2017). This will let you know how many buyers should be in each buying group, so you can remove the excess.

For example, in Figure 9.5 we can see the higher survey responses for four times (which is a typical error for a month time frame) and the deficit in responses in three and five times. The NBD fit shows what the results should look like. Further calculations can use these 'smoothed' NBD estimate figures.

Figure 9.5: Example of category buying frequency distribution with an averaging error at four weeks and the NBD fit estimates to show the expected distribution

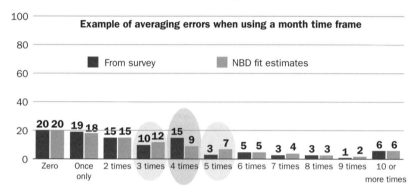

Buyer level fix

If you want to classify individuals into buying weight groups for reporting or further analysis, then use the identified errors to more intelligently group categories together. Cancel out errors by combining the under and over estimations (as per Ludwichowska 2013).

For example, if there is a bump at ten times and a deficit at nine times and 11 times, then group nine, ten and 11 times together rather than, say, eight, nine and ten times. This process will remove the arbitrary distinction between (in this example) nine, ten and 11, when many of the *ten times* responses are really nine or 11 times.

Table 9.4 shows an example of how to combine groups. The deficit in three- and five-times buyers compensates for the excess in four-times buyers. The combined three-, four- and five-times buyer's group has less total error than the more detailed data. Once you work out what needs to be fixed, ongoing measurement can use the shorter scale with the combined category groups.

Table 9.4: Example of how to combine buyer groups to compensate for survey response errors

Full distribution				Truncated distribution with error prone groups combined			
	Survey %	NBD est. %	Diff.		Survey %	NBD est. %	Diff.
Zero	20	20	0	Zero	20	20	0
Once only	19	18	0	Once only	19	18	0
2 times	15	15	0	2 times	15	15	0
3 times	10	12	-2	3–5 times	28	27	1
4 times	15	9	6	6–9 times	12	14	-2
5 times	3	7	-4	10 or more times	6	6	1
6 times	5	5	0				
7 times	3	4	-1				
8 times	3	3	0				
9 times	1	2	-1				
10 or more times	6	6	1				

How to use category and sub-category metrics

The focus of this chapter is about getting better quality metrics for use in screening and buyer classification. It is difficult to get a sense of category growth from online surveys because usually the survey sample is drawn from a panel that is not representative of the population. To be able to see category growth or decline in number of buyers in category buying metrics, you would first have to recruit a sample representative of the total adult population, then get category buying as a proportion of this sample. This is a very inefficient approach for ongoing CBM tracking.

If category growth/decline is a major issue, then a separate stand-alone study is a better approach to gather this information. You can either use syndicated services or collect your own data to track changes in category penetration and any effect on the category buyer profile.

If you have sub-categories where you collect penetration and buying frequency, you can use this data to understand market structure at sub-category level, by applying the Laws of Growth.[4] For example:

- *The Double Jeopardy law* helps you understand loyalty to sub-categories, detect any unusual loyalty metrics (e.g., Singh et al. 2008), and map how sub-categories grow and decline.
- *The Duplication of Purchase law* helps you understand how sub-categories compete and detect if there are any clusters of sub-categories that have excess or deficit in sharing. This can be useful for designing multi-sub-category promotions and understanding the potential impact of any individual sub-category growth on other sub-categories (e.g., Wilson et al. 2019, Anesbury et al. 2021). Table 9.5 shows an example of this analysis for a sub-set of non-alcoholic beverages that reveals excess sharing between fruity and cola soft drinks, as well as natural and flavoured mineral water.

Table 9.5: Example of a Duplication of Purchase table for sub-categories (excess sharing examples highlighted)

	% of buyers who also bought ...									
	Fruit juice	Cordial	Milk	Cola NS	Cola	Fruity SD	MW (N)	MW (FI)	SW	Iced tea
Fruit juice		61	60	43	46	47	44	46	37	27
Cordial	65		63	47	47	49	37	43	30	28
Milk	64	65		42	46	46	41	39	32	26
Cola NS	62	65	56		39	49	41	47	31	26
Cola	69	66	63	40		58	40	44	33	30
Fruity soft drinks	72	71	65	51	60		43	49	37	32
Mineral water	68	53	58	43	41	43		60	43	23
Min. water (FI)	72	63	57	51	46	50	61		38	31
Spring water	73	58	60	43	44	48	57	48		24
Iced tea	67	66	62	45	51	53	38	49	30	
Average	68	63	60	45	47	49	45	47	35	27

---

4   See Chapter 1 or *How Brands Grow 1 & 2*.

- *Brand buyer profiles* analysis helps you understand if any sub-categories have a substantively different customer base that might either limit growth and/or indicate that your brand needs to have a variant in that sub-category or risk being locked out of its sales (e.g., Trinh et al. 2009).

Together these areas can help you understand sub-categories dynamics within a larger category.

Chapter summary

For a CBM tracker, the most useful people to survey are category buyers. The influence of category users who do not buy (e.g., children, partners and gift recipients) will still be visible through the brand memories of category buyers.

Before you design category and brand buying questions, get some basic facts on how the category is bought:

- *Category purchase frequency* – How often is the category bought and how this changes over different time periods, to help determine the most useful timeframes for measurement.
- *Repertoire size* – How many category buyers use only one brand? How many use two, three, four etc, to help understand how to construct brand buying questions.
- *Shopping behaviour* – Where is the category bought from and what are the different environments where people shop, to identify any that may need to be highlighted to get accurate buying behaviour.
- *Category growth dynamics* – Is the category growing via adding new buyers (penetration), such that the category buyer definition might need to be expanded to also include likely future purchases.

The key category metrics to measure are the following:

- *Category penetration* – To ensure an appropriate sample is recruited for interview, and to capture the penetration of any sub-categories. Using a reference time frame before your target time frame improves the accuracy of your results.

- *Category buying weight* – To be able to classify respondents into lighter or heavier category buyers. The recommended approach is to use a number or purchases, either of the category or across sub-categories, as this is the most memorable repeated behaviour.

The next chapter examines brand buying, where many of the same measurement principles apply, but the presence of many different competitors opens up new challenges and opportunities.

10

Brand Buying

JENNI ROMANIUK

While every tracker contains questions about brands the category buyer has bought, poor design often limits the value that can be extracted from this data.

This chapter shows how to develop a set of more robust brand buying questions and how to use this data, and highlights some common design/wording mistakes to avoid.

Two benefits from collecting brand buying data

A well-designed set of brand buying metrics provides you with the context to better interpret buyer responses and brand level category buyer memory (CBM) scores, and it can be a source of brand buying behaviour insights for categories where the recorded brand buying data is absent, insufficient or expensive.

Benefit 1: Provide context for CBM metrics

What brand of mobile phone do you have? What do you know about this brand? You know what it looks like, how it feels in your hand, how other people react to it, how long the battery lasts and whether it is easy to keep clean. In short, you have a set of stored memories about this brand of phone that have formed through your ownership.

To get into the mindset of a brand non-buyer, think about a brand of mobile phone you have never bought—here are a few brand names if you are stuck: Xiaomi, HTC, Nokia and Google Pixel. What do you associate with these brands? Take a minute to write down your associations. Associations with brands not bought will be fewer and harder to retrieve than the associations for a brand you have bought.

Non-buyer memories for a brand come from 'indirect' experiences such as advertising, watching other people interact with the brand in real life or on social media, publicity or Word-of-Mouth. With sufficient attention, these indirect experiences can build memories among a brand's non-buyers (Simmonds et al. 2020).

These indirect experiences also affect brand buyers. Brand buyers are:

- able to more easily process information from advertising (Simmonds et al. 2020)
- two to three times more likely to notice advertising from a brand they bought (Harrison 2013, Vaughan et al. 2016)
- two to three times more likely to receive Word-of-Mouth about the brand (Uncles et al. 2010, Romaniuk and East 2016).

Many brand buyers get both direct and indirect experience to build their memories, while a brand's non-buyers have fewer sources to build new memories or reinforce existing ones. Therefore, buyers of a brand are more responsive to questions that call on brand memories than brand non-buyers without (more recent) direct brand experience.

But that's not all …

Just to complicate things, non-buyers of your brand are buyers of competitor brands. This means your brand's non-buyers have (often many) more memories for the competitor brands they have bought. In our mobile phone example, some non-buyers of Samsung are buyers of Huawei. The few weak memories these category buyers have for Samsung compete with their many stronger memories for Huawei. Separating out responses for a brand's buyers from non-buyers allows us to better understand the brand memories of both.

We need brand buying questions that can easily, and as accurately as possible, classify category buyers into brand buyers or brand non-buyers. Analysis that controls for brand buying also improves the sensitivity of metrics, as it reveals when there are different changes over time for specific sub-groups (e.g., see Chapter 2, Table 2.5 that shows brand awareness metric changes over time across buyer groups). All of this serves to improve the quality of CBM metrics.

Benefit 2: Provide buyer-centric brand performance metrics

Collecting comprehensive buyer-centric metrics has always been a problem for non-household packaged goods categories. Marketers in categories such as services, durables and luxury products have long 'made do' with survey data, as have categories with large out-of-home consumption (e.g., confectionery and alcohol) or in emerging markets where household panels are rarely present or comprehensive. Collecting better quality brand buying data will benefit marketers in all the categories that rely on survey data.

But wait, there's more … The proliferation of sales channels means even mature household grocery staples now find it a challenge to capture comprehensive buyer-centric data. The growth of e-commerce and direct-to-consumer channels means even if you can source your buying data from a commercial household panel, the cost, range and flexibility of survey data means it can be a valuable addition to your insight tools.

A well-designed survey can get key brand buying metrics to:

- test for the Laws of Growth, such as Double Jeopardy and Duplication of Purchase, and detect any new deviations
- evaluate brand performance over time (growth in brand penetration and loyalty)
- check the performance of new brands
- provide a quick snapshot of brand buying patterns prior to entering new categories or countries.

Key brand measures: Brand penetration and brand buying weight

To achieve these two benefits from collecting brand buying data, we need these two measures:

1 *Brand penetration* – To classify category buyers into brand non-buyers and brand buyers.

2 *Brand buying weight* – To classify brand buyers into heavy and light brand buyers.

When combined, these two metrics give you most of information you need to understand a buyer, brand or a category of brands.

Measuring brand penetration

On the surface, measuring brand penetration seems quite straightforward—just ask whether someone is a brand buyer or not. In durable or subscription categories you can ask if someone is a customer of a brand, owns a brand's product or has bought a product in the past.

There are two types of classification questions:

1 Having an ongoing (financial) relationship, such as *Do you currently subscribe to Netflix? Which company do you have a life insurance policy with?*

2 Having bought in the (recent) past, such as *Have you bought Jack Daniel's whiskey in the last three months? Where have you been on holiday in the last 12 months?*

In categories where buying is a series of repeated transaction events, as with category buying, you need to decide on a time frame to consider someone a current brand buyer.

What time frames are useful?

As discussed in Chapter 9 on category buying behaviour, the time frame depends on the inter-purchase buying frequency of the category. The more frequent the buying, the shorter the recommended time frame. There are practical modelling reasons why you might want your brand buying time frame to be the same as the category buying time frame (for example, if wanting to fit the NBD-Dirichlet model; see Goodhardt et al. 1984). See the suggested time frames for different categories in Chapter 9 for initial suggestions.

From a memory perspective, remember that buying any one brand is equal to or less frequent than category buying. This means you might need a longer time frame for brand buying if you want to, in a subsequent question, separate out heavier and lighter brand buyers. For example, you might ask category buying over a three-month time period but want brand buying over a 12-month time period. Any extension of the time frame needs to consider the potential for memory degradation and the memory load on the respondent. The best option is to collect the same time frame as for category buying, and then add an additional time frame as needed for classification or analysis. However, I have seen questionnaires that collect annual, quarterly, monthly *and* weekly buying. This feels like overkill and places an unnecessary memory burden on respondents.

Make brand buying easy to remember

We want to make it as easy as possible for the buyer to remember any brand buying event to minimise errors due to light brand buyers forgetting that one purchase (Nenycz-Thiel et al. 2013). Here are some steps to achieve this objective:

1 *Provide a list of possible brands, in alphabetical order*

Provide a list of brands as it is easier for category buyers to recognise a brand rather than recall it from memory. Providing a list helps capture less commonly used brands within a commonly used category or all brands in a less commonly used category.

Putting the brands in alphabetical order makes it easier for people to find the brands as they do remember them, and therefore give a more complete answer. Chapter 3 explains when images are beneficial in Brand Awareness measurement; use the same approach here.

2 *Provide a reference time frame to reduce telescoping*

Remember from Chapter 9, telescoping is when someone answers for a longer time frame than specified in the question because our memory markers of time are unclear. As with category buying, employing a bounded recall question design and having a reference time frame before the target time frame will help reduce telescoping (Ludwichowska 2013).

3 *Avoid using any other questions as filters*

All survey questions have errors—sampling error, respondent error, measurement error, coding errors—that all pop up in various forms throughout any piece of research. To minimise the risk of compounding errors, do not make your brand buying questions conditional on any previous responses.

Measuring brand buying weight

Once you have established someone is a buyer, the next objective is to measure relative buying weight. Buying weight can be assessed three ways:

1 *How often* (e.g., purchase frequency, buying rate) – How many times a brand is bought within a time frame.

2 *How much* (e.g., share of category requirements, share loyalty) – The amount (volume or value) of buying that involves the brand relative to competitors also bought.

3 *How long* (e.g., % of new buyers, % of repeat buyers) – The length of time a buyer has been buying a brand in the past or will do so in the future.

How often?

How often refers to how many times the brand is bought in a time period. It can range from one to the maximum times the category was bought. This question is akin to category buying frequency, so the same guidelines apply, but the importance of getting accurate responses from light brand buyers is even more pronounced, given their important contribution to brand growth and decline.

Brand buying frequency typically occurs with much lower frequency than category buying. Therefore, the lower ends of the scale (buying one or two times) are even more important in brand buying questions.[1] While brand buying frequency can be prone to the same averaging and rounding errors evident in category buying frequency, these errors will only apply to very big brands and/or very long time frames. Correct any errors that emerge using the steps recommended in Chapter 9.

It might seem more efficient to ask penetration and frequency at the same time, on a scale from 0 to maximum frequency. However, screening via a brand penetration question reduces respondents' cognitive load as they are only asked the more difficult-to-answer question of *how often/much* for a smaller number of brands. This is, of course, predicated on following the steps to ensure a relatively accurate brand penetration question.

---

1   The exception is sole brand loyalty, but they are also light buyers (Sharp and Romaniuk 2021b), which means they also use the lower part of any frequency scale.

Durables or services, where a product or service is bought once a year (e.g., annual renewal) or on a less frequent basis, can use the following two metrics:

1 *Number of products/services* – In a broader category that consists of sub-categories of products or services, where it is possible to purchase different brands (e.g., take out different products such as credit cards, home loans and investment accounts from different banks), you can create a 'number of products/services' loyalty metric to capture how many times, out of all the product opportunities, the brand is bought.

   This metric is only useful when there is a relatively consistent list of competing brands for each sub-category. Otherwise, you risk a brand getting a low score because of its product range, not the behaviour of its buyers.

2 *Repeat buying* – In subscription or durable categories you can also draw on the past to capture brand choice across multiple purchase occasions over time. If you have a category where using another brand means they have defected (i.e., closed their account with the prior brand), then you can ask for the brand used in that category 12 months ago.

When combined with the information on the brand currently used, this can identify buyers that have changed brands for that product category. This can then be used to calculate:

- *annual defection rates* – % of customer base that left the brand
- *annual acquisition rates* – % of customer base that is newly acquired in last 12 months.

You can also identify the competitors that acquired your brand's lost customers/source of your brand's newly acquired customers and use the Duplication of Purchase law (Goodhardt and Ehrenberg 1969, Sharp and Romaniuk 2016) to identify if there is excess loss/gain with specific competitors (for an example of this in Business-to-Business banking, see Romaniuk 2021c).

How much?

Buying weight can also be quantified by the volume or value of products bought. However, as volume or value assessments are not discrete events, they are rarely remembered well unless the purchase was unusual. For example, buyers often fail to recall the price of everyday supermarket purchases, even shortly after selecting the brand (Dickson and Sawyer 1990). This makes it unlikely they will remember how much they spent on any brand sufficiently to calculate value with any accuracy.

Time spent is another volume type of metric that is hard to capture as time passes quickly if the experience is enjoyable. As Einstein supposedly quipped, '*When you sit with a nice girl for two hours you think it's only a minute. But when you sit on a hot stove for a minute you think it's two hours. That's relativity.*'[2] Asking someone how long something took is going to generate a response biased by the enjoyability of the experience.

How much metrics such as volume, value or time spent are better captured via observation research or passive recording of the behaviour rather than via recollection in surveys. The good news is that frequency of buying responses can be converted into a *share of buying* metric. To do this, you need to:

1 add up purchases the buyer base makes for that brand; then
2 add up purchases that the brand's buyer base makes across all brands in the category; then
3 calculate the share that the buyer bases' brand purchases are of the same buyers' category purchases across all brands.

This won't be perfect, particularly in categories where products differ substantively in volume or prices per item, but it will provide a relatively good starting point. You can then overlay volume or value differences as needed for specific brands.

What about the use of 'most often bought' as a quick way to get buying weight?

---

2   This quote was recorded in his *New York Times* obituary as his quote from 1929, but there are many variations.

An often-used quick, single response question to measure of buying weight is 'which do you buy most often?' This is not recommended for the following reasons:

- The 'most often' approach lacks precision because of the interaction with buying frequency. A brand's *most often bought* base is going to be a mix of 'statistical' light buyers of the category who only buy this brand and 'genuine' heavy brand buyers who buy the category and the brand often. This creation of such a heterogenous buying group makes the classification of questionable value in analyses or reporting.

- It also assumes each buyer has a single brand bought more often than other brands. However, a five times category buyer might buy two brands each twice and another brand once. Either of these two brands could be the 'brand bought most often' response. In testing across three packaged goods, up to 35% of category buyers who bought the category at least twice did not have a single brand they bought more often than other brands. Therefore, this question introduces further error into the data.

If the buying frequency question is separated from the brand penetration measure, each buyer only has to answer for a small sub-set of brands. The richness of the information collected from this separate frequency question makes the additional effort worthwhile.

How long?

Think about a brand you buy from that is relatively new to you. Can you pinpoint the date when you first started using them? While writing this I tried to remember the first time I used Airbnb. My estimate was 2017, but when I looked at my profile on the site, it was actually 2015. Evidence from looking at new brand buyer memory structures shows that most of the time, even buying a new brand is a relatively small event in someone's life (Sharp and Romaniuk 2016). Memorability is less accurate for common events or events from a long time ago. Therefore, brand tenure measures in surveys are best used to identify recent new brand buyers (for your brand or competitors), where the memorability of the event is slightly higher because the buying event is *both* new and recent.

Measuring recent brand uptake provides data that can be used to calculate each brand's acquisition rate and see if any brand is acquiring new customers at a rate faster than expected.

Common mistakes to avoid when measuring brand buying weight

Here are some approaches that pop up in questionnaires that, although well-intended, reduce the quality and usefulness of brand buying data.

Imprecise questions

The effort to make the question 'friendly' can introduce ambiguity and imprecision. Labels/terms that could mean very different things to different buyers are difficult to interpret. Examples of such wording include:

- Which brands do you regularly buy?
- Which brands do you typically buy?
- Which brands do you buy on occasion?

Words like regularly, typically and on occasion do not work in a category where buyers have vastly different category and brand buying rates. A heavy buyer's *regular* brand buying might be once a week, while a light buyer's *regular* brand buying might be once a quarter. This creates an un-useful heterogeneous group of '*regular*' buyers.

Standardising the number of purchases

Another approach to measure buying frequency over time is to ask all category buyers for the brands bought over a specific number of purchases, such as the last three, five or ten purchases. This approach also ignores that purchase rates vary across the category/brand buying population. The last three purchase occasions for a heavy category buyer of toothpaste could be three months, while for a light buyer of toothpaste it could cover two years.

Asking about specific past purchases can improve memory, particularly for big 'event' purchases such as holidays, cars or smartphones. If you take this approach, then still only include purchases within a time frame such as last five years. That means some category buyers might only answer for one purchase, while other category buyers might answer for about five purchases. Allowing for the category purchase rate variability ensures your data better reflects real-world market conditions.

Providing rate-based categories

Another approach is to ask people to estimate how often they buy a brand or category and then provide different rates per time period, such as:

- daily
- three or four times a week
- once a week
- a few times a month.

This is a poor penetration measure *and* a poor frequency measure, and so it is unclear what you could do with the data other than simply report the results.

Future buying

By now you are probably thinking, it is all well and good to capture the past, but it is the future I am most interested in. How can I tell if my marketing activity improved the chance that someone will buy my brand in the future? Another common measure to track is purchase intent, which captures people's intentions/desires/plans to buy a brand in the future. The question typically looks like this:

> Q: How likely are you to choose each of these brands next time you buy <insert category>?
>
> With five response categories: (1) Definitely will buy, (2) Probably will buy, (3) Might or might not buy, (4) Probably will not buy, (5) Definitely will not buy.

The genesis of this type of measure is 'The Theory of Planned Behaviour' (Ajzen 1991), which assumes that a buyer has plans to buy certain brands that they can share when questioned. The response you get from a future behaviour measure at the time of survey is the respondent's best estimation of the future after the survey. However, this estimation can be undone by random life events. For example, you might have no intention to buy a new refrigerator in the next 12 months, but then your fridge breaks down.

Improving future behaviour estimations

The following factors improve the accuracy of measures (Kalwani and Silk 1982, Morwitz et al. 2007, Wright and MacRae 2007):

- Asking about common behaviour such as buying an established product/brand rather than a change in behaviour such as buying a new product/brand.
- Asking about durable categories that are typically higher value and have more memorable buying processes rather than a low value, less memorable packaged good.
- Using larger sample sizes to reduce the impact of stochastic (random) variation.
- Using a shorter time frame so there is a lower chance that a rare event will happen to disrupt estimations.
- Asking a purchase probability question, such as the Juster scale (Juster 1966), which performed better in a meta-analysis compared to relative accuracy to purchase intent questions (for the meta-analysis details, see Wright and MacRae 2007).

The Juster scale

Frustration with the inaccuracy of purchase intent measures led to the development of purchase probability scales, which do not assume the presence of any latent plans (Juster 1966). Instead, this approach asks category buyers to calculate an 'on the spot' likelihood that a future event will occur during a specified time frame. The Juster scale is one of the most well-known purchase probability scales (e.g., Juster 1966, Brennan 2004). Table 10.1 shows an example of Juster scale question wording for those interested in using this approach (adapted from Juster 1966).

However, the reality is buyers are better at looking back than looking forward, so any future estimations of behaviour should be taken with a 'grain of salt' as the best estimates at the time of questioning, but easily dissuaded by unforeseen circumstances.

Table 10.1: Example of wording for the Juster scale

QJUSTER. What is the chance you will buy <insert brand> in the next <insert time frame>? I'd like you to answer based on the scales below where 0 means you have no chance or almost no chance of buying <insert brand> in the next <insert time frame>; while 10 means you are certain or practically certain you will buy <insert brand> in the next <insert time frame>. You can think of the numbers as chances out of 10, where 3 is a 3 in 10 chance and 7 is a 7 in 10 chance. Therefore, using the scale below, what is the chance that you will buy <insert brand> in the next <insert time frame>? *Please select an answer on the scale below*	CODE
No chance, almost no chance [1 chance in 100]	0
Very slight possibility [1 chance in 10]	1
Slight possibility [2 chances in 10]	2
Some possibility [3 chances in 10]	3
Fair possibility [4 chances in 10]	4
Fairly good possibility [5 chances in 10]	5
Good possibility [6 chances in 10]	6
Probable [7 chances in 10]	7
Very probable [8 chances in 10]	8
Almost sure [9 chances in 10]	9
Certain, practically certain [99 chances in 100]	10

Chapter summary

This chapter covered how to measure two key aspects of brand buying:

- *Brand penetration* – To identify if a category buyer is a brand buyer.
- *Brand buying weight* – To quantify the value of each brand buyer.

Brand penetration is useful for context-setting when interpreting CBM measures, as its differences in past direct experience with the brand results in major differences in the baseline brand memories across category buyers.

A brand buying weight measure is useful to separate out lighter from heavier brand buyers. We can then detect if we are keeping up fresh memories among all types of brand buyers, but particularly the more vulnerable lighter brand buyers.

Of the three approaches (how often, how much or how long) in transactional categories such as consumer packaged goods, the recommended approach for measuring brand buying weight is asking *How many times did you buy brand X in <insert time-period>?* Collecting this information at category level as well means you can also calculate a share loyalty figure for each brand.

For categories where category buyers can buy different brands for several different sub-categories, you can calculate a *number of products* buying weight measure by summing together each sub-category's brand penetration results.

In all category types, you can create a short term 'how long ago' measure to identify recent new brand buyers. This can be used to calculate a brand's new buyer acquisition rate.

The penetration and buying weight measures collected here can also serve as inputs into testing the Laws of Growth, such as Double Jeopardy and Duplication of Purchase (see Chapter 1 for more detail).

Finally, if you want to collect the estimations about future behaviour, the Juster scale is a better approach. But just remember, category buyers find it hard enough to remember what they have bought in the past, so we need to be realistic and temper our expectations about the ability of category buyers to accurately estimate what they will buy in the future.

11

Measuring Exposure to Marketing Activity

JENNI ROMANIUK

To understand the potential of marketing activity to have an impact on category buyers, we need to consider the hurdles that any activity faces before it can be effective. These hurdles form the basis of measurement that checks for exposure to marketing activity in a category buyer memory (CBM) tracker. The first hurdle is it needs to be noticed and the second hurdle is that it needs to be linked to the right brand(s). Having relevant messages is also important, but this can and should be checked before launch and so is not needed in a CBM survey.

Therefore, it is the Effective Reach (i.e., that category buyers noticed the activity) and Correct Branding (i.e., that category buyers can link the activity to the brand) that are the focus of measurement. This chapter will cover how to collect and use this information.

What have you done for (the brand) lately?

To understand the effects of the brand's marketing activities, you need to know if these activities have gained category buyers' attention. While there are schools of thought that advertising can work without conscious attention (e.g, Heath 2000), this will be difficult to discern with a survey. In a CBM tracker it is more realistic to focus on category buyers' memory for activities.

This is at once simple and difficult. It is simple in that it is just a catalogue of activities and asking category buyers about them. It is difficult because of the gaps between what category buyers notice and what they remember. We need a questioning regime that captures memory for the exposure as easily and accurately as possible.

Marketing activity measurement in a tracker

We want to make it easy for people to accurately remember if they have been exposed to the brand's marketing activity. This means tapping into recognition memory, rather than relying on recall. Advertising recall measures (e.g., *Which brands have you seen automobile advertising for recently?*) suffer from the same cue and retrieval limitations of unprompted measures discussed throughout this book and are not recommended in a brand tracking instrument.

Selecting activities to include in a survey

Any activity of scale should be included in the CBM tracker. Brand tracking surveys only sample a small proportion of the category buying population. This means any marketing activity needs to have the potential reach to make it worth including. This is not a major disadvantage as the bigger reach activities can impact the greatest number of category buyers, and so have the greatest potential to impact sales. Indeed, if you find most of your marketing activities do not have enough reach to be capable of proper testing in a CBM tracker, then perhaps your marketing team is wasting too many resources on very small, low impact activities.[1]

To set the tracker up well, you also need to include major activities from competitors. Otherwise, the target brand is too obvious to the category buyer and you risk priming effects where the category buyer

---

1   Some specifically targeted initiatives with low reach, but need accessibility (e.g., communicating improved access for people with disabilities), might need alternative ways to determine impact among that specific community.

recalls a brand for one stimulus and then is more likely to respond with that same brand for other stimuli, particularly if there are common creative threads. Large reach stimuli from competitor brands breaks up the correct brand response. You want at least as many competitor stimuli as you have for your brand, but a two to one ratio will more effectively mask the brand of interest.

Remember you are designing for the category as much as possible. Therefore, if you have six stimuli to test, ideally you want 12 notable activities from competitors. The questions about the stimuli are very simple to answer, so having up to 20 stimuli is not over-taxing.

Effective Reach

The first step to measuring marketing activity is to isolate different creative copy and create still images, video or audio files that do not have the brand present but include the dominant, unique elements of the creative. This can be a scene, person or sound—any elements that are likely to trigger memory for exposure to the creative, separate to the brand.

If you have executions that follow a similar creative thread, they are best tested as one creative unless there are clearly different elements that can separate the two for category buyers. This avoids overloading the respondent with multiple iterations of very similar stimuli, and subsequent reduced accuracy due to incorrect execution attribution.

Creating stimuli for execution testing also requires a clear understanding of the brand's Distinctive Assets to avoid inadvertently including a Distinctive Asset as part of the test stimuli. You want to avoid including Distinctive Assets because these appear across multiple executions and so increase the risk of misattribution, whereby the respondent remembers the Distinctive Asset but from a different execution. Including Distinctive Assets in the Effective Reach test also makes it difficult to separately test Correct Branding.

Once you have the fully de-branded stimuli, it is simply a matter of exposing the category buyer to the stimuli and asking if they remember exposure in the time period that covers when it was in-market and asking a yes/no response.

Correct Branding

After the category buyer confirms they remember the creative execution, the next step is to check if they also remember the brand being advertised. This is essential for building Mental Availability (Vaughan et al. 2020). We want to know if the brand was embedded in memory as part of the communication, which means unprompted recall is the best approach. Do this, as standard, to allow for multiple brands being mentioned, given the prevalence of dual branded advertising. Also include a check box for 'don't know' to discourage guessing. If any brand is encoded effectively, it should be just as memorable as the creative.

Prompted approaches that just involve recognising the brand name are too easy. This is also likely to bias category buyers towards ticking a brand response (because that is the 'right' answer), even though they might have no brand linked to the creative in memory. Approaches that only offer multiple brand options without a 'don't know' option to force responses exacerbate the likelihood of guessing.

After previously explaining the drawbacks in unprompted approaches for Brand Awareness and brand attribute measurement, you might be wondering why the switch here to advocating unprompted measurement. The reason is here we are testing if the brand is encoded in memory in response to a specific stimulus, and so unprompted measurement with the stimulus as the retrieval cue gives us the best chance of separating the link to that specific stimulus from any others in memory.

Approaches that ask respondents to evaluate branding quality on a scale are not measures of memory encoding. These are not recommended for this purpose.

Trouble de-branding?

Executions or activities that cannot be separated from the brand (e.g., the brand's website) can be tested with the brand using the same memory for exposure question, but after the de-branded executions and their Correct Branding questions are complete.

Key metrics

- *Effective Reach %* = n of people remembering exposure/total sample
- *Correct Branding %* = n of people who correctly named the brand/n of people remembering exposure
- *Branded Reach %* = % reach * % Correct Branding

For example, if 73 people out of a sample of 400 remembered exposure for the ad:

Effective Reach = 73/400 = 18%

Then if 24 of the 73 people correctly named the brand:

Correct Branding = 24/73 = 33%

Therefore:

Branded Reach = 18% * 33% = 6%

This means in this example 6% of the total sample of category buyers remembered the ad *and* the brand being advertised.

If the stimulus is not de-branded:

Branded Reach = % recognised the stimuli with branding

How to use the data: There are many analyses you can do with this data, both within a wave of tracking and over time. This section highlights some analyses we have found useful.

Diagnostics for low-impact activities

If the branded recall is low, these two metrics help us understand why the marketing activity did not register in category buyer memory. The Effective Reach and Correct Branding metrics also allow us to see if either is more at fault for the low score:

- In the prior example, reach was 18%. We can compare this score against estimates from the media plan. If we did not spend a great deal of money, 18% might be a good score. But if the media plan was estimating 40% reach, then something went awry.
- Correct Branding was 33%, so we can ascertain that two in three category buyers we paid to reach did not remember the brand name. This is something that should be fixed before any more money is spent on this activity.

Total Branded Reach metrics

A CBM tracker is less useful to diagnose problems with individual creative as by the time you get the results it is too late; you have already spent the media budget. So any insights you get for individual creative is a nice bonus. The key value of including execution specific questions into the tracker is to calculate a more robust Total Branded Reach metric than simply asking an overall advertising recall or recognition question.

After you calculate the Branded Reach for each activity, you can combine the variables to see how many category buyers were reached by at least one. This can then be converted into a binary variable: 1 = Branded Reach and 0 = not Branded Reach.

Total Branded Reach = % category buyers who remembered *and* correctly branded at least one of the brand's marketing activities

If you are in a category where Word-of-Mouth is prevalent, you may want to include category buyers who received positive Word-of-Mouth about the brand in this equation.

Fuel brand example

Table 11.1 shows an example of this exercise for a fuel brand[2] that engaged in TV advertising (two executions) and an outdoor campaign (similarly themed so tested as one execution) in the United Kingdom. Effective Reach and Correct Branding tests revealed the performance metrics listed in Table 11.1.

Table 11.1: Individual marketing activity metrics for a fuel brand in the United Kingdom

	Effective Reach %	Correct Branding %	Branded Reach %
TVC 1	27	58	16
TVC 2	17	60	10
Outdoor	17	89	15
Total Branded Reach			24

---

2   The advertising and the data are real, but the brand is confidential.

For this test we interviewed the same sample[3] of n=686 respondents over two waves, six weeks apart. During the first wave interview, respondents who had a car and bought fuel were asked their penetration and frequency of buying different fuel brands in the six weeks prior to that first interview. Respondents were recruited from an opt-in panel, but did not know they would be re-contacted at a later stage. At the second interview, they were asked again about buying frequency of different fuel brands (including the target brand). Later in the survey they were asked Effective Reach and Correct Branding questions for the three stimuli.

From these questions we calculated change in Brand Purchase Frequency for different exposure groups. In this test we can look directly at the effect on frequency of purchasing that brand of fuel, because we have a short enough time frame to remember purchases, enough advertising expenditure for the advertising to have wide exposure, it is a category that is bought frequently, and there are many different brands easily available to buy. This combination of characteristics is rare, but helpful for this example. You also do not need to use this method on an ongoing basis to get value from the Effective Reach and Correct Branding data—this is just to illustrate why they are valuable to track and the importance of analysis by buyer group.

Table 11.2 shows that across the whole sample, the Total Branded Reach exposure group had the biggest positive effect (+0.3), followed by the Reach only group, who remembered an execution but not the brand (+0.1). Those with no memory for any advertising exposure had no change in Brand Purchase Frequency. However, when we split into buyer groups:

- this change is most notable only among very light/non buyers (+0.7) who fall in the Total Branded Reach category, where there is virtually no difference between the Effective Reach only and No exposure group
- brand buyer results are all negative and suggest the greatest decay with no exposure, but the small sample sizes make it difficult to confirm these differences between groups.

Therefore, it is clear the results for buyer groups follow very different patterns and combining the two group together weakens the ability to detect advertising effects.

---

3   This individual level longitudinal data is not necessary in tracking but is helpful in R&D as it removes sampling error that is pronounced when comparing different cross-sectional samples.

This reiterates the point made throughout this book that to get the most effective assessment of the impact of any CBM metric, split the sample into brand non-buyers and buyers, and compare impact within those buyer groups. That will not remove all the confounding factors, but it will remove several major ones.

Table 11.2: Results for testing the relationship between Total Branded Reach and changes in Brand Purchase Frequency

Exposure groups	All category buyers	Very light/ non-brand buyers	Brand buyers
No exposure	0	+0.2	−1.1
Effective Reach only (no brand identification)	+0.1	+0.2	−0.2
Total Branded Reach	+0.3	+0.7	−0.7
ANOVA sig. Test	p=0.08	p<0.001	ns

Food product example

In another example for a food product, Mental Penetration (MPen) is systematically higher for three brands' buyers compared to their non-buyers, but for each brand's buyers MPen is close to 100%. It is in the non-buyers where we see brand size differences.

Separating out the two groups (Figure 11.1) we can more clearly see the difference between those with Total Branded Reach compared with those not remembering any branded marketing activities on non-buyers. The difference is apparent for three brands of different market share.

Even if you do not want to conduct this analysis, tracking the Total Branded Reach across all your key marketing activities can provide you with a benchmark to understand if you can hope for more changes in CBM metrics because your Total Branded Reach is higher, or expect less change because your Total Branded Reach is lower than previous waves.

Often brand health trackers contain a range of other advertising assessment metrics. These are often measures that should have been collected prior to launch and fixed if there was a problem (e.g., Messaging and Creative quality assessments). There is little value in cluttering up a tracker with this information.

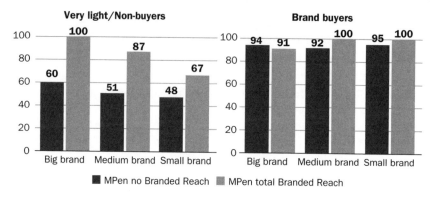

Figure 11.1: Example of results comparing MPen results for exposed versus unexposed across buyer groups for a food product in the United States

Chapter summary

This chapter showed how to identify buyers with Branded Reach, which enables you to assess whether the marketing activity has had sufficient widespread impact to change CBM metrics.

The key metrics are:

- *Effective Reach %* = n of people remembering exposure/total sample
- *Correct Branding %* = n of people who correctly named the brand/n of people remembering exposure
- *Branded Reach %* = % reach * % Correct Branding
- *Total Branded Reach* = % category buyers who remembered *and* correctly branded at least one of the brand's marketing activities.

This helps set expectations as to the effects of marketing activities and opens the door to more detailed analysis of the effects of marketing activities. It also enables you to diagnose if reach or branding quality needs improvement.

Category buyers do need to split into buyer/non-buyer segments for more sensitive analysis.

12

Word-of-Mouth

JENNI ROMANIUK

Word-of-Mouth (WOM) is peer-to-peer sharing of content (e.g., words, images, sounds or videos) about brands. Long acknowledged as an influential form of communication, research as far back as the 1950s has examined WOM generation, processing and contribution to brand value (e.g., Brooks Jr. 1957). Growth in social media usage and the portability of electronic devices provide today's category buyer with a wider range of opportunities to give and receive WOM about brands. This has increased marketers' interest in WOM measurement and metrics.

WOM differs from paid influencer or celebrity endorsements because the source is someone personally known to the recipient. This chapter focuses on this unpaid or 'organic' WOM[1] and explores the different aspects of WOM measurement, as well as the contextual factors that help you get more value from WOM results.

What is WOM?

WOM is any part of personal conversation where a brand features. This conversation can be a clear recommendation to act (e.g., *You should buy a*

---

1   Paid influencers and celebrity endorsements are better assessed with the approaches covered in Chapter 11.

Nespresso machine, it makes such good coffee), or it can be a passing comment that includes a brand (e.g., *I'm glad I bought the extra carton of Happy Eggs last week, the kids wanted scrambled eggs again this morning, it's the fifth time this week!*).

When you meet someone who you know, what do you talk about? Yesterday, did you talk about your family, your job, sports events, politics, the cute video you saw on social media, what's for dinner that night …? What about brands?[2] How often did brands come up in your conversations?

For a normal person, most of their conversation is *not* about brands, and the bit that is about brands is fractured over the many brands they know and is a small part of a wider conversation. This means when we ask about WOM for any brand or category, we are typically asking people to remember a relatively rare and insignificant event. These two characteristics create measurement challenges we need to overcome when designing WOM questions.

Even when just a passing comment, WOM can still impact buyer behaviour. Given our cluttered lives, any comment about any brand can be influential, if the right person remembers it at the right time. Therefore, it is worthwhile, at minimum, benchmarking WOM levels to assess its potential influence in your category. But before we get into the nitty-gritty of the measurement issues, let us first step back and review the key dimensions of WOM to better understand what we are measuring and its value to include in a category buyer memory tracker.

The story of WOM

The story of WOM has four chapters, but not all WOM chapters are relevant all the time. You really need to *choose your own adventure* based on your objectives. Every piece of WOM has two participants: a giver and at least one receiver. *The giver* generates the WOM. Therefore, measuring WOM from the giver-side can help us identify:

- who produced the WOM
- why the WOM was given
- how much WOM was produced.

---

2 The ones you do not work for/with.

The receiver is the agent of any action due to the WOM. Measuring receiver-side WOM helps identify who the WOM reached and its impact.

WOM can also be positive or negative in valence. This is also important to track because:

- for givers, the triggers of positive WOM (PWOM) can differ from the triggers for negative WOM (NWOM)
- for receivers, the direction of influence changes as PWOM generally encourages brand choice, and NWOM generally discourages brand choice.[3]

Therefore, capturing whether the WOM is positively or negatively orientated helps understand the likely impact of the WOM and how it can be dampened or encouraged as benefits the brand.

Linking the 'why' with the 'who'

Whether you want to speak to givers or receivers depends on your objective(s). For example, there is no point asking givers about the impact of their WOM, as this is something recipients determine. Equally, there is no point asking receivers what triggered the WOM as they are unlikely to know what was in the giver's mind when they spoke. Table 12.1 shows the links between the key reasons for measuring WOM and the appropriate research audience.

Table 12.1: Reasons for WOM measurement

Audience	Objective
Givers	What triggers WOM production in the category?
	To what extent have our WOM generating activities worked?
	Has a new advertising campaign generated WOM?
	Has the publicity around unusual/rare events, such as a takeover or product recall, produced WOM?
Receivers	Attribution modelling – WOM impact/revenue
	Does any particular WOM message have more impact than others?
	Is PWOM delivering incremental reach over marketing activities?
	Is NWOM discouraging potential buyers or causing current buyers to defect?
Both	Benchmarking to understand expected levels of WOM

---

3   We found around 3% of WOM has a contrary effect, where PWOM actually discouraged purchase. This is because WOM is inextricably intwined with the giver and, in the words of one recipient who said the PWOM made her less likely to watch a TV program, 'It's from my mum and I don't like what she likes'.

Givers gonna give …

The giver generates the WOM, but what triggers the giver? Extensive research in this area finds the brand's actions stimulate only a small part of WOM production. WOM mainly comes from social and environmental influences (e.g., Mangold et al. 1999; East et al. 2015).

There are two broad types of triggers for PWOM and/or NWOM: those arising internally from within the giver and those emerging externally from the environment:

- **Internal** triggers come from the giver's actual or desired emotional state. These triggers include:

  - *To share feelings of satisfaction/dissatisfaction with a brand interaction* (e.g., you share your experience about having great/poor food at a restaurant to bond with others).

  - *To want to feel helpful* (e.g., to help someone you know who is going out to dinner to decide where to go, you recommend a restaurant or discourage them from going somewhere you feel would be a bad option).

  - *To enhance oneself in the eyes of others* (e.g., to impress someone you tell them about your positive or negative experience of a dinner at an exclusive restaurant).

  - *(For NWOM only) To reduce anxiety after a negative experience* (e.g., you recount the experience of a particularly rude waiter to someone to 'get that off your chest').

  - *(For NWOM only) To extract vengeance against the brand* (e.g., you share an experience where the restaurant owner was rude to you to discourage others from going there as a way to get payback).

- **External** triggers come from the giver's environment including other people, the location or the brand. These triggers include:

  - *When asked* (e.g., someone asks you for a restaurant suggestion or about your experience dining at a particular place).

  - *The topic came up in conversation* (e.g., you are conversing with someone about London, and you contribute by sharing your experience at a restaurant in London).

  - *Seeing advertising* (e.g., you see an advertisement for a restaurant, and it prompts you to talk about the advertising or a past brand experience at that, or some other, restaurant).

- *Needing something to stimulate the conversation* (e.g., you are sitting with someone and bring up a recent experience at a restaurant to break the ice).
- *Had a noteworthy brand experience to share* (e.g., you share the experience of being given a free glass of champagne at a restaurant because it was something unusual).

Therefore, it is not just the brand's actions that stimulate WOM. The giver's emotions, the recipient's current state, and the environment also affect WOM production. This means you cannot claim or blame the brand's activities for all WOM generated. If you want to attribute a brand's WOM to a specific marketing activity or outcome, you need to remove other influences as much as possible. Then you will be in a better position to more effectively interpret the brand's WOM score.

Past brand buying matters when giving WOM

It is probably getting a bit predictable now, but for given WOM, past brand buying is an important contextual factor. We rarely give WOM about brands we have not directly experienced (East et al. 2007). If a brand has more buyers, it has more people 'in the market' to give WOM, which means it typically gets more WOM than smaller brands with fewer buyers. It is normal to have a straightforward relationship between buying and PWOM. The more buyers a brand has, the more PWOM is produced for the brand, relative to other brands in the same category (Uncles et al. 2010).

For NWOM it can be bit more complicated. The correlation between NWOM and brand penetration can be lower than for PWOM because:
- most brands perform as they should on most occasions, so fewer buyers have a negative story to tell/reason to advise against any specific brand (East et al. 2017); therefore, lower scores overall can mean lower variation between brands
- a brand's lapsed buyers are most likely to give NWOM (Romaniuk and East 2016), because they are in the non-buyer group, so can distort the correlation between penetration and NWOM.

However, as Figure 12.1 shows, there is often still a positive correlation between NWOM and Brand Penetration. Just do not be dismayed if in your category NWOM's correlation is a bit lower than for PWOM, particularly if NWOM is rare.

Figure 12.1: PWOM and NWOM by brand penetration in banking category, Australia

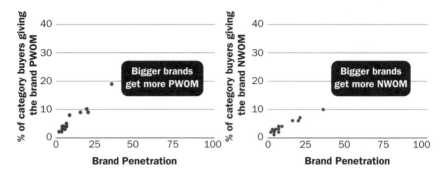

Giver-side WOM measures and metrics

In any time period, the same person can give PWOM and/or NWOM on multiple occasions to different recipients. Therefore, we need to capture both WOM penetration, or the number of WOM givers, and WOM frequency, which is the amount of WOM produced by each giver. This gives us the capability to calculate the given WOM per 100 category buyers (in line with East et al. 2007), which standardises WOM volume over different sample sizes:

* *Given PWOM volume per 100 category buyers* = PWOM penetration *
  PWOM frequency, normalised to response per 100
* *Given NWOM volume per 100 category buyers* = NWOM penetration *
  NWOM frequency, normalised to response per 100.

The time frame

As the giving of WOM is often a minor, infrequent event, use a shorter time frame so while WOM volumes might be low, responses are more accurate. One month suits most categories; three months might be useful for larger/riskier purchases such as white goods, cars, holiday destinations or financial services. You can extrapolate this number to estimate figures for a longer time frame.

Interpreting the metrics

Brand buyers are more likely to give PWOM or NWOM, which means bigger brands typically get more PWOM and NWOM than smaller brands. This again highlights that smaller brands suffer more from lack of attention than negative sentiment. Therefore, brand penetration levels provide a useful context to generate expected brand levels of given WOM. This process can help you determine if your WOM is higher or normal for a brand of its penetration in that category.

When WOM penetration is multiplied by the average frequency (Column 5 in Table 12.2), it is possible to calculate a volume per 100 category buyers. Converting the raw WOM volume scores to a volume per 100 makes it easier to compare between brands, over time, across categories and with NWOM.

Table 12.2 shows an example of the modelling needed to identify the expected level of volume of PWOM per 100 category buyers for a brand. In this market, a model of *Expected PWOM Vol per 100 = 1.35 * PWOM Vol per 100* provides estimations with a +/−2.5 pp Mean Absolute Deviation. This means we can see ING gets more PWOM than expected (+7), while ANZ gets less PWOM that expected (−7). If we managed one of these brands, we could then investigate the source of these deviations.

Table 12.2: Given PWOM for financial services—example of metrics and modelling results (two largest deviations highlighted)

PWOM	Pen. (%)	Actual Given PWOM (%)	Given PWOM Frequency	PWOM Volume per 100 category buyers*	Expected PWOM Volume per 100**
Commonwealth	36	19	2.6	48	49
ANZ	21	9	2.5	22	29
NAB	20	10	2.6	25	26
Westpac	16	9	2.6	24	21
ING	9	8	2.6	19	12
St. George	7	4	2.5	11	10

PWOM	Pen. (%)	Actual Given PWOM (%)	Given PWOM Frequency	PWOM Volume per 100 category buyers*	Expected PWOM Volume per 100**
Bendigo	7	5	2.6	14	9
Suncorp	7	5	2.7	13	9
Bankwest	6	3	1.9	6	8
BoQ	5	4	2.3	8	6
HSBC	4	4	2.7	10	6
Macquarie	4	3	2.7	7	5
BankSA	4	2	1.9	4	5
ME	3	2	2.2	5	4
Beyond	2	2	2.6	5	3

*(n WOM * freq)/sample size)*100, **model is Expected PWOM Vol per 100 = PWOM Vol per 100 *1.35

Receivers gonna receive (sometimes) ...

When I think of WOM recipients, I think of my old dog Honey. At the time of writing this she is over 15 years old and has poor eyesight, but still loves to play fetch. Unfortunately, because she can't really see, the toys I throw often whizz right past her, unnoticed. Such is the story of most WOM. Therefore, we need to talk to the (potential) recipient if we want to ascertain if the WOM had an impact on their behaviour. For WOM to impact recipients' behaviour, there are two conditions to be met:

1 *Did it get the receiver's attention?*

   Think of all the things someone has said that you didn't hear because you were daydreaming, or all the social media posts you have missed because you scrolled too fast or didn't check in that day—oh wait, you can't, because you can't remember what you didn't notice. On top of that, think all the times you remember someone recommended a new TV show, but you can't remember what the show was called, or who recommended it. Just because a giver gives WOM, it does not mean the receiver received the message. You could ascertain if the receiver noticed the WOM by asking, but that is only the first step. To impact behaviour, the recipient also needs *room to move*.

2   *Is there 'room to move'?*

Not everyone receiving WOM is able to act on that advice/comment. WOM needs to reach a 'movable' audience, one that can change their buying propensities upon receiving the WOM. Everyone's chance of buying a brand can be plotted on a probability scale from 0% to 100% (in line with the Juster scale from Chapter 10; Juster 1966). This initial probability determines the extent of any impact of received WOM.

For PWOM to have an impact, receivers need to be able to go up …

If someone is at a 10 out of 10 chance that they will do something, then PWOM will be ineffectual as the recipient had already decided to act prior to receiving the WOM. This happens quite often because WOM is *conversation* and topics of conversation usually centre around the mutual interests of the people conversing.

For example, my sister might speak to me about a new Spanish restaurant because she knows I like Spanish food, but not with her daughter Gabby, because she is not interested in Spanish food. But the same interest in Spanish food that led her to talk to me about the new restaurant also meant I was already booked in to eat at the restaurant. So, her PWOM is ineffectual because I was already at the top end of the probability scale, and I couldn't move up the scale. It is only when someone is undecided or unaware that PWOM can have a positive impact on their propensity to buy the brand.

For NWOM to have an impact, you need to be able to go down …

Think of all the things you have very little or no chance of doing. I have no chance of watching any of the *Real Housewives* … series, running a marathon, or selecting a vegan restaurant when it is my choice. So, telling me how bad any of these things are is falling on futile, rather than fertile, ground. But it is not just the things I do not like. There are many other brands in any category that I have zero probability of buying. For example, I have zero probability of becoming a customer from most banks. I am not in the category for most banking products and have no probability of buying from the vast majority of the 100 or more banks that offer those banking products. If you say something negative about any of those banks, the consequences are also nothing. I can only downgrade my probability of buying the brand upon hearing NWOM when I am undecided or close to buying.

Figure 12.2: Example of different WOM effects based on baseline probabilities for PWOM and NWOM for restaurants, United States

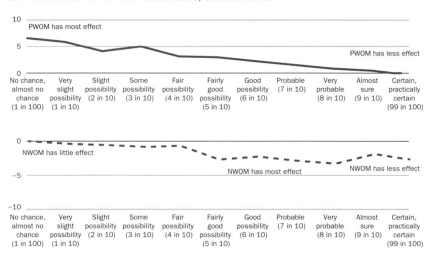

Receiver-side WOM measures

The key measure for WOM receipt is penetration, or how many category buyers received at least one instance of WOM in a specific time period:

- *Received PWOM penetration* – % of people who received PWOM about the brand at least once
- *Received NWOM penetration* – % of people who received NWOM about the brand at least once.

The time frame should be the same as given WOM so you can easily compare the two[4]. You can also collect the frequency of receiving WOM; however, in my experience this provides little additional return for the effort.

Key metrics across buyer groups

To isolate the key metrics, again separate category buyers into brand light/non-buyers and brand buyers. Then calculate the following metrics for each buyer group/WOM type:

---

4   To date we have not tested if the same process of asking a reference time frame before the target time frame improves the accuracy of WOM measures. This is because it is difficult to verify WOM figures. However, it is an area for future research when the opportunity presents itself.

- *PWOM received by non-buyers* – signals a potential to increase Mental Availability
- *NWOM received by buyers* – signals a potential to develop negative sentiment and lead to greater brand rejection.

This approach emphasises the sub-set of category buyers with the greatest potential to act on each type of WOM (see Figure 12.3 for example metrics from the banking category). These benchmarks can be used as a baseline to quantify any lift in WOM should there be an event that might cause an increase (e.g., PWOM increase due to a new product launch; or NWOM increase due to a product recall). Over different events you can establish a database of expected WOM lifts under different conditions.

Figure 12.3: Example key metrics for WOM

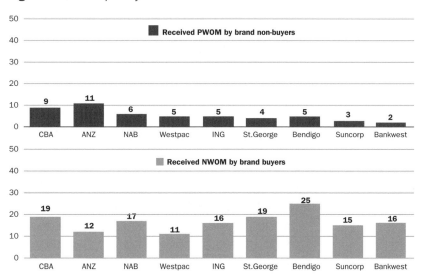

It is possible to do more complex analysis of WOM effects. One useful approach to follow is to calculate revised probabilities after WOM exposure (as described in East et al. 2008). However, this is more appropriate for an in-depth analysis of WOM influence than ongoing tracking.

Can I just monitor brand mentions on social media?

Given the prevalence of social media networks and the amount of engagement online, often social media monitoring is suggested as a low cost, easily available alternative to surveys. Some of the many challenges with using this form of measurement include:

- it is only given WOM, so it is only one side of the story, and you have no understanding of any recipients, so you cannot determine any likely impact
- it is also only a small part of WOM given, as WOM is still much more often given in a face-to-face context (Engagement Labs 2021)
- you have to infer if it is positive or negative, which can introduce error due to misinterpretation. For example, in online comments about chocolate brands was the phrase 'RIP Snickers'. No, the person did not want Snickers the chocolate bar killed off, but rather someone was mourning their hamster called Snickers. Similarly, the meaning of words such as 'sick' vary with age cohorts.

And drawing only on online data assumes that people's conversation online mirrors their conversation offline. Anyone on Twitter might question that assumption!

Willingness to recommend/Net Promoter Score

It is impossible to have a chapter on WOM without mentioning the Net Promoter Score and its underlying 'willingness to recommend' measure. This should not be used as a proxy for WOM because:

- it is only asked of customers, so misses WOM from non-buyers; thus underestimating NWOM that is most likely to be elicited by lapsed buyers (Romaniuk and East 2016)
- the Net Promoter Score metric focuses on the promoters (9–10) and detractors (6 or below) and excludes the passives, who are responsible for giving most PWOM (Romaniuk et al. 2010)
- it is highly correlated with customer satisfaction metrics, so there's no need to measure it if you already have a measure of customer satisfaction (East et al. 2011).

This measure lacks face validity as a WOM measure. Do not use it as a substitute for measuring actual given or received WOM.

Can I just measure WOM as an attribute?

Another relatively common attempt to measure WOM is via the creation of WOMish attributes, which are then measured in the image battery along with other brand attributes. Examples of WOMish attributes:

- *A brand lots of people are talking about.*
- *A brand you would recommend.*
- *It is recommended by family and friends.*
- *Has a buzz about it.*
- *Heard people say positive things.*
- *Heard people say negative things.*

This form of measurement lacks specificity. There is no link to a time frame or even a specific WOM event, and therefore it is difficult to interpret or act upon the results.

An exception is *recommended by <insert expert relevant to category, such as dentists or vets>*, which can be a Category Entry Point or baseline competency in high-risk categories (e.g., infant pain relief). In this case you are not measuring actual WOM but the category buyer's perception that the brand is endorsed by experts. This perception of an endorsement provides credibility/confidence for a risky purchase. When a brand gets unusually high responses, this can usually be traced to the use of experts in advertising or social media.

Chapter summary

WOM measurement involves capturing:

- instances of PWOM and NWOM; from
- both givers and recipients; and
- contextual factors to properly interpret the results.

You can establish benchmark metrics for any category to get a sense of what normal WOM for that category looks like and to set up the programming for ad hoc measurement that might be needed. However, in most categories, WOM data collection can be just tracked or reported on an event basis, triggered when something happens that could disrupt normal WOM patterns. Only if WOM volume is high or volatile is it worthwhile to pay sustained attention to WOM metrics.

The measurement audience depends on your objective. Anything related to WOM production (who, how much, why) needs giver-side measurement. However, anything related to WOM impact (additional unduplicated reach, attribution modelling, the impact of different types of WOM) needs receiver-side measurement.

Finally, remember your brand is only responsible for a portion of its generated WOM. So, if you want to attribute WOM to a particular marketing activity, make sure you first strip out as many of the other WOM triggers as possible.

Key WOM metrics are as follows:

Given WOM	Received WOM
PWOM Volume per 100 category buyers	PWOM Penetration among non-buyers
NWOM Volume per 100 category buyers	NWOM Penetration among buyers

13

The Rise of
the Machines?

ANNE SHARP AND JENNI ROMANIUK

With so much data available online, and some of it about brands, maybe it is unnecessary to survey category buyers to measure brand health. Perhaps our human intelligence-gathering systems can be replaced by smarter machines, incorporating artificial intelligence and machine learning to 'scrape', analyse and synthesise the wealth of information from the online universe.

Linked to this is the question of how brands can harness communities that self-select their interest in the brand via their own online behaviour. These people are ready and willing to give their opinion, so perhaps they can replace paid online panellists.

In this chapter we look at the ability of common types of publicly available online data to gauge brand health and replace category buyer surveys. We cannot discuss all possible uses of online data—that would be a book in itself! Rather, we focus on the feasibility of capturing the information needed to cover category buyer memory (CBM) tracker areas through using data scraped from online activity. Then we examine opportunities to use brand communities, where the biases in these participants can be a research asset.

Online data 'scraping'

Technology now allows us to draw together information from a wide range of online sources, including search terms, reviews, social media posts and online brand communities. The promise of this technology, when compared to category buyer surveys, includes the ability to:

- track the brand 'in the wild' and observe how people talk about brands, rather than the questions we ask dictating the topics of discussion
- gather data from large volumes of people rather than a smaller sample of online panellists
- get data quickly, and so learn quickly when events happen
- draw on the latest technology and reduce human error.

However, despite these potential advantages, there are three big limitations to the data collected via online data scraping:

1 Many forums are closed to data scraping, with private chats and some social media sites unable to be accessed. Therefore, the available data is only the conversations people choose to make in public forums.

2 You do not know the source of the comments, so are blind to the declarant's history with the category or brand. Therefore, it is difficult to isolate information from different buyer groups.

3 You only get declared questions or information, which is going to be biased towards buying contexts that are the unusual and hence newsworthy or difficult, such that someone needs help/advice. The good, but unremarkable, Chobani yoghurt someone had for breakfast is not going to be worthy of an online comment.

But can we get useful insights, even with these limitations? Let us critically examine the information available across key CBM areas.

Brand Awareness

In Chapter 3 we covered how the key metric for Brand Awareness is prompted Brand Awareness from the brand's non-buyers. While many companies offer services to track brand mentions, you cannot split the data into brand buyers and non-buyers. However, perhaps you can assume that if buyers are at 100% prompted awareness, you can also reasonably assume that non-buyers, who often have prompted Brand Awareness much lower than 100%, are the primary source of any change in brand mentions over time.

The following are four concerns with this idea:

1   The brand's presence in someone's brain is only 'visible' when that person types the brand name. This misses those who are aware of the brand but have nothing to talk about or share. This brand memory presence/online expression of that presence gap needs to be as small as possible to be confident you are getting an accurate measure of Brand Awareness.

2   To be an identifier of category membership, you need to know the cue that stimulated the brand mention. Going back to our Russell Stover example in Chapter 2, unless you know that online mentions are in the context of chocolate, it is unclear if changes in brand mentions are actual changes in Brand Awareness. This is particularly challenging for brands with a strong presence in an existing category and who are looking to enter a new one.

3   It is unclear what actual 'awareness' is measured. The memory processes for brand mentions vary according to the source. For example, to search in Google, someone must first think of the brand then type it into Google, which is unprompted recall. However, commenting on a post that someone else has written about the brand requires recognition of the brand. This makes it difficult to know what you are capturing when these responses are combined.

4   Buyers notice more marketing activity than non-buyers (e.g., Vaughan et al. 2016) and marketing activity can stimulate conversation online. So, the assumption that changes in brand mentions can be tied to an increased presence of the brand in the memory of non-buyers requires a questionable leap of faith.

These issues make it difficult to interpret or act on the results from any monitoring of Brand Awareness via online mentions.

Generating Category Entry Points

Another possible use of online comments is to generate a list of Category Entry Points (CEPs). As discussed in Chapter 5, online search terms and discussion about the category skew to the *unknown, unusual* or *shareable*, rather than the typical, everyday contexts that comprise the brand's core revenue. Therefore, online data is unlikely to constitute a complete source of CEPs for tracking.

The same limitations constrain the use of online data to assess brand performance on CEPs. Any search on CEPs brings up a whole range of non-brand related items. Wading through this list to get to brands is not going to be an easy or cheap task. However, the online tracking of comments could be an avenue to identify new contexts/uses/pain points in the category. This can be a source of innovation to evolve the brand or company portfolio.

Brand attitude and Word-of-Mouth

Word-of-Mouth (WOM) refers to peer-to-peer communication. In an online context, these are comments posted on social media networks and are referred to as electronic WOM (eWOM). These comments can be collected and analysed for content (what is said) and sentiment (positive or negative). The sentiment aspect of coding of online comments is where eWOM and brand attitude cross over. The comments reveal how people feel about brands (brand attitude) and those same comments comprise content that is shared with others online (eWOM).

First let us consider the content from sources such as social media posts and online reviews. Analyses of the distribution of online reviews reveal a polarised, positively skewed distribution (Schoenmueller et al. 2020). Most reviews are very positive and some reviews are extremely negative, but very few are in the middle. This is at odds with the natural distribution of brand attitude (Chapter 8), where most people feel neutral or mildly positive about most brands. For example, Figure 13.1 compares the survey distribution of brand attitude for fast casual chain restaurants with the distribution of ratings from customers across three review sites. The review sites are seven times more negative and 1.5 times more strongly positive than a survey distribution.

Figure 13.1: Comparison of survey and review site attitude distributions for five fast casual restaurants, United States

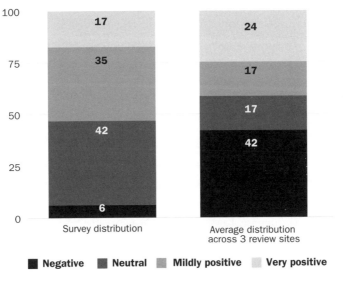

This leads to a distorted view of the brand's attitude: that everyone is either very positive or very negative. A parallel can be drawn to what we see in community engagement exercises. The people who feel strongly, known as the 'squeaky wheels', contribute as they have something to say, but the 'silent majority' live up to their label. This ends up with views that are important, but not a reflection of how the general population feels.

There may be value in tracking any negative eWOM and identifying any themes that emerge from the comments. If you can establish benchmarks, then sudden jumps in negative sentiment will be easy to detect. By reviewing the comments, you might be able to identify the cause of the jump. This might be of value if you are involved with a category or brand where controversy is common. However, this only deals with given negative WOM and (possibly) given positive WOM. It is impossible to tell who received the WOM, so you cannot tell whether it reached the key audiences to influence behaviour (see Chapter 12).

Therefore, in summary, we cannot see a good argument for replacing a well-designed CBM survey with online data sources. The data is too incomplete and flawed. Now let us cover some areas where marketers can get more value from online discussion/comments.

Brand community panels

The digital world provides numerous forums for like-minded individuals to cluster. An organisation can draw on this herd-collecting quality to build its own in-house panel of brand buyers for research purposes. For example, there are insurers, banks, video streaming services, beauty brands and department stores with panels of their brand users to regularly consult for topics such as feedback on new product ideas or recent customer service experiences.

These communities can involve contributors to brand-owned social media properties such as Facebook sites, Reddit forums, followers of brand on Twitter, visitors to the brand's website, or a separate panel of customers recruited and maintained by the brand's marketing or insights team. Examples include Lego Ideas, DuoLingo Incubator or Salesforce Trailblazer. Typically, recruitment for panels comes after engagement with the brand. For example, Amazon Prime has its Amazon Preview where pre-recruited viewers are given access to selected upcoming content. The website describes the group as follows:

What is Amazon Preview?[1]

Amazon Preview is an exclusive opportunity for entertainment fans to help shape Movies and TV Series. Once you've accepted our invitation, we will email you opportunities to view and provide feedback on entertainment projects – before they're available to anyone else. We'll share concepts, storyboards, test movies and even television pilots with Amazon Preview members and use the feedback we collect from them to make entertainment projects better.

What do I get for participating in Amazon Preview?

First and foremost, you'll get an exclusive behind-the-scenes look at the television and movie projects. Your feedback will help us improve these projects for all Amazon Customers. From time-to-time, we may also offer prizes and giveaways to Amazon Preview members as a thank you for your participation.

---

1   https://www.amazonpreview.com

The people invited to comment are selected based on their viewing preferences and past viewing behaviour, making this a very private (members sign non-disclosure agreements) way to gain early feedback. The rewards reflect those common for company-run communities— product related, in this case seeing exclusive content early, and intangible, in this case feeling like you are part of the product creation process.

As these have rewards that centre on the product, brand communities have inherent biases and limitations that will affect research results:

- The panel will naturally attract the more involved, knowledgeable and heavier buyers of the brand and category, who gain the most from being a panel member (Nelson-Field et al. 2012). Medium or light buyers feel they have less to contribute and stand to gain less from their contributions, so are less likely to take the time and effort to be a panel member. Therefore, brand communities are skewed to people who know more, buy more and usually feel more positively about the category/brand.
- You also only see a partial snapshot of these members' activity in the category. The research tends to focus only on what the buyer is doing with a specific brand. This is usually the brand that 'owns' the panel.
- Brand non-buyers are typically not included, nor do they have any motive to join without a non-brand-related incentive. This bias leads to an overrepresentation of the popularity of the brand in any research.

It is critical to factor these biases into your interpretation. Treat any brand community results as the best-case response from the brand's 'fan' base. These biases can, however, be a strength for types of research where heavier engagement is an asset. Here are some examples of research areas where feedback from brand communities can add value.

Pre-testing changes to communications

Providing this community with early access to new directions in the product portfolio, marketing communications or public relations initiatives can act as a pre-test. You can test the new direction is acceptable to existing users.

Feedback from this community can help avoid a costly mistake, such as making a change in packaging so radical that existing customers struggle to recognise the pack, which could compromise their ability to find the brand on-shelf; or changing the logo and getting a backlash from customers.

Pre-testing new launches such as line or category extensions

The first buyers of new line extensions are likely to be heavy buyers of the brand (Tanusondjaja et al. 2016, Trinh et al. 2016). Therefore, another use of a community of heavy brand buyers is to trial new launch concepts or products prior to a full launch. This ensures you get feedback from likely early adopters who are also most likely to buy and talk about it, and so are crucial for a new launch's early success (see also Grasby et al. 2022).

An example of this usage is the Royal Automobile Association (RAA) in South Australia that recently broadened its product portfolio away from just being an organisation to call upon for roadside assistance when your car breaks down to offering loans, travel products and real-time fuel pricing information. Before making this change, RAA could draw upon its in-house panel to ensure these extensions were consistent with what people felt this organisation could and should offer.

Gaining insight into more difficult research questions

A brand community allows you to develop deeper relationships and ask more in-depth questions from community members. With prolonged engagement you can also ask more complex tasks of respondents and give them information to reflect on. For example, you could ask them to upload photos or videos to help you better understand how they use your product, or to keep a diary to ensure more accurate capture of hard-to-recall and measure behaviours. You can also collect longitudinal data that helps you to build an understanding of how your brand buyers evolve or fluctuate in terms of behaviour or attitudes over time.

Talking to hard-to-reach customers

An in-house panel can also help you to reach hard-to-find users. For example, Woolworth's supermarket has 'Woolies Customer Faces' who are 'a small group of customers who represent different types of people that shop with us and will help Woolworths make decisions with our customers front of mind'. The supermarket uses this sort of approach to find customers who buy organic, have very young children in the household, have a plant-based diet etc. The low incidence of these sorts of customers means they can be very time consuming and expensive to find in commercial panels.

A replacement for mystery shopping

In-house panels offer an easy way to gain follow-up feedback on specific events. For example, after in-store or online retail interaction, community members can get a 'Care to Share' email asking them to rate aspects of the shopping experience. With this sort of research, you are really focused on what your buyers did with your brand, and so the biases to your users are less of a shortcoming. An example of this is Uber. After taking a ride or having an Uber Eats delivery, you may receive an email along the lines of:

> Thank you for being part of the Uber community, and for your continued use of services provided by Uber. As part of Uber's commitment to ensure our offerings improve your experience, we are inviting you to take a quick survey to share your thoughts.

Sometimes, the reward may be with an allied brand rather than with the organisation which is the focus of the research. To continue our Uber example, it may be a $5 Amazon gift card.

Idea generation from your most invested

Finally, a review of the conversations from online brand communities and asking questions of the community can leverage the knowledge and involvement of members. This insight can provide ideas for new product or service development or other changes to improve the offering.

An example in Figure 13.2 is LinkedIn inviting their active members to tell them more about what they consider the most important things to be in a job, so that they can develop more services to support those seeking new hires or roles.

Figure 13.2: Invitation from LinkedIn communications

> Thanks for being a member of LinkedIn! We would
> like to invite you to participate in a research study
> to understand the most important things in a job.
> Your feedback will be crucial in helping companies
> attract, motivate and retain top talent.

Risks associated with building brand communities

It takes considerable resources to build and maintain a brand community. Therefore, any benefits associated with brand communities need to be weighed against both the costs and the risks. If the community does not feel their voice is being heard, or if the community is shut down, there could be a backlash against the brand from its most ardent supporters. The brand communities also are a considerable drain on resources and so the opportunity cost of what else could be done with those resources needs to be factored in. Over time, communities may also become even more unrepresentative of your users due to their constant exposure to the category and your brand through the research.

Finally, the logistics of panel management are also challenging. When does someone become 'lapsed'? How do you engage in targeted recruitment to adjust for the loss of some types of panel members? For example, younger panel members might be harder to keep interested. These challenges make it worthwhile thinking carefully before deciding to build your own brand community.

Chapter summary

Despite the promise of cheap, immediate insights from mining online brand mentions, it is difficult to see how online data mining can replace direct questioning of category buyers. This data tends to be biased to positive and negative extremes, and to the unusual or difficult events. Comments cannot be attributed to a category or brand buyer type, nor can the comment recipients be profiled. This limits the usability of the data.

However, the volume of negative online comments can provide a benchmark to indicate jumps in negative sentiment, and the content of those comments can provide clues as to the cause of the jumps. This can help you to quickly catch and address issues if you are in a more volatile category.

The other source of data online is via brand communities, which can be built and maintained by the company. These communities usually comprise heavier users of the brand/category and more involved brand buyers, which means their reactions and responses are not representative of the wider category or brand buying population. However, this respondent skew can be used to research advantage for:

- pre-testing any changes to your brand or communication to check for buyer acceptance
- pre-testing new launches or category extensions among the audience most likely to buy first
- building longer term relationships to gain answers to more complicated research questions
- building a base of hard-to-reach customers to enable you to get their opinions quickly and cost efficiently
- replacing mystery shopping research
- sourcing ideas for new product and service innovations.

Still, it is often necessary to supplement information gained from an online brand community with a more representative sample. This data also says nothing about how to attract new category or brand buyers. Therefore, online pre-existing data and brand community data is best utilised alongside survey methods to fill specific data information niches.

14

What about Physical Availability?

MAGDA NENYCZ-THIEL AND JENNI ROMANIUK

The first chapter of this book covered the fundamental empirical laws that help us understand how brands grow. These 'Laws of Growth' lead us into the two key areas for businesses to manage in the quest for sustainable, profitable growth, which are:

- *Mental Availability* – being easily thought of in buying situations
- *Physical Availability* – being easy to find and buy.

This book has several chapters on Mental Availability, but is Physical Availability something to include in a category buyer memory (CBM) tracker?

In this chapter we outline suggestions for monitoring Physical Availability. While there are some areas that can involve a CBM tracker, most of the information you need comes from other sources. Here we provide guidelines and frameworks to get you started collecting this data. As this is ongoing work within the Ehrenberg-Bass Institute, the objective with this chapter is to give you some suggestions you can implement now, and get you excited for our future insights on this topic.

What is Physical Availability (again)?

Physical Availability is about making the brand *easy to find and buy*. *Easy to find* is about implementing tactics to help the brand stand out in often cluttered sales environments, while *easy to buy* is about implementing tactics that make it easier for category buyers to transact. This includes developments such as creating Presence where there was none (e.g., setting up vending machines in locations that don't have a retailer Presence), innovations (e.g., Amazon's one-click purchase) or removal of impediments (e.g., accepting PayPal to reduce the fees for overseas customers) or addressing an important entry level price point (e.g., introducing a lower cost ad-supported TV streaming service to the product Portfolio).

The following are the three pillars of Physical Availability (Nenycz-Thiel and Romaniuk 2021, Nenycz-Thiel et al. 2021).

1 *Presence* – Being present where buying is or could happen—at the key channels and retailer chains, but also sometimes where the buyer is but retailers are not, such as the back of taxis/ride share vehicles or vending machines in remote locations.

2 *Portfolio* – Being buyable across those options above—covering the key parts of the category (such as price tiers or pack sizes) across people, occasions and over time.

3 *Prominence* – Being easily found in any sales environment—such as a physical store, e-commerce, m-commerce or social commerce.

Each of these three pillars has some fundamentals areas to track, which are common to most categories, even though the specific measures and metrics might change. These fundamental areas are the focus of this chapter.

Presence

Managing Presence involves taking steps to try to make the brand present wherever the buyer is looking to buy. Having Presence helps the brand capitalise on Mental Availability built outside of the sales environment. If the brand is not there, the buyer most likely has other brands that they can buy instead. Measuring Presence therefore involves capturing the extent of the brand's distribution; that is, the coverage of the key and emerging channels and intermediaries (retailers, brokers). You want to check if the brand:

- uses current channel investments wisely to provide the optimal coverage for the money spent
- maintains adequate investment in existing channels to avoid putting core product/service sales at risk
- appropriately invests in newer channel options so the brand is not left behind as these grow
- avoids wasting resources by over-investing or investing too early in newer sales channels that have nascent revenue streams but are not yet profitable.

That is some balancing act!

Now, many of you working in consumer-packaged goods might say *'We buy this data from the third-party providers, so we don't need to measure this ourselves'.* Indeed, in *some* categories and *some* countries, agencies can provide this information. However, even in developed markets this information often does not cover the possible universe of Presence. Retailers can only provide their data, while third-party providers can only provide the data that retailers are willing to provide to them. In some markets this means no discounters, while in others, no impulse and often a lack of visibility on many e-commerce channels. If you are blind to at least 30–40% of category Presence from specific channels/retailers, you are making decisions based on incomplete information.

Having your own mechanism for keeping track of this helps you control your metrics. It won't be perfect, but you will know the limitations. Therefore, even if you get this data from an agency, you might find it useful to map what you get against what is recommended for the category to identify and address the shortfalls.

Presence management: Suggested tracking metrics

To assess a brand's Presence performance, you need to know the following:

1 *Sales outlet universe* – What are the key channels and retailer and service outlets within these, where the category is or can be sold? This tells you the potential universe of Presence options.

2 *Category sales* – How big is the category at each of the channels/ retailers and what is the current dynamic of the category sales there? This tells you the current and near future opportunity within each Presence option.

3 *Coverage* – Where is your brand present? This reveals the brand's current performance and gaps in Presence. You can keep this simple by just mapping the brand as a binary yes or no; or you can map the Presence of different Portfolio options. The level of complexity is up to you, but we recommend starting simple and adding more layers rather than starting overly complex and struggling to fill it all in!

The list of sales outlets will vary by category. Here are examples from different category types (Table 14.1).

Table 14.1: Examples of different channels to consider for different categories

Pet food	Home loan	Vacuum cleaner
Hypermarkets	Brick and mortar branches	Electrical retailers
Supermarkets	Brand websites	Department stores
Discounters	Brokers	Discounters
Club stores	Online marketplaces	Club stores
Convenience stores	Mobile apps	Specialist vacuum retailers
Specialist pet retailers	Financial advisers	Online marketplaces
Direct-to-consumer websites		Brand webs
Online marketplaces		Direct-to-consumer websites
Veterinarians		
(Many of these channels have online and in-store options to consider)		

Table 14.2 illustrates how to set up a table to collect and calculate benchmark metrics. The overall aim is very simple. Calculate the universe of possibilities, identify which of those possibilities are new, then calculate how many of those possibilities the brand currently has covered.

Most of this data can be obtained by desk research (free and paid) and utilising sales representatives where available. An annual update will make sure it keeps up to date with category changes. Your own Presence data map can highlight gaps or areas of over-investment to investigate further, as well as growing channels that might need greater investment.

Once you have set up the basics, you can choose to get more sophisticated and measure the quality or the depth of distribution. This could include the share of shelf, the position of the brand in an online marketplace, or the rank order of the brand in a web search. However, these additions should be secondary as the more complicated something is, the less likely it will be used or maintained. Your priority is to get a *good-enough* read on whether the brand has a widespread Presence now and is well-positioned to keep this widespread Presence in the future.

Key metrics to monitor are:

- *% channel coverage* = n outlets brand is available in that channel/total outlets in that channel with any category brand available (column 6 in Table 14.2)
- *% overall market coverage* = n outlets brand is available/n total outlets all category brands are available (bottom of column 6 in Table 14.2)
- *% Presence in new outlets* = n outlets brand is available in outlets emerging in last 2 years/n outlets emerging in last 2 years per channel (column 8 that are new outlets in Table 14.2)
- *% overall new outlet coverage* = n outlets brand is available in outlets emerging in last 2 years/n outlets emerging in last 2 years (bottom of column 8 in Table 14.2).

Portfolio

The role of the Portfolio management is to try to develop a suite of products that cover the market as much as possible—across people and occasions and over time. We want to provide potential buyers with a suitable option in any moment, if it is profitable for us to do so. For example, if a buyer's CEP for the dog food category is concern about their dog's weight, there is a lower calorie option, while if a buyer enters the category looking for something to help improve the quality of life for their 15-year-old dog who has arthritis, there is an 'older dog healthy' option. If your brand does not have a suitable option in either of these situations, it might lose the sale to a competitor, thereby laying waste to Mental Availability building efforts.

The 'right' Portfolio balances covering category buyers' current needs and setting the brand up for the future. This means treading a delicate

Table 14.2: Outline of Brand A Presence mapping at a channel level for a pet food brand

Sales outlet Universe	Category sales			Brand performance				
	% of category sales generated in a channel	Total # of outlets in market	Total # of outlets new in last 2 years	# Outlets with Brand A Presence	Brand A % coverage of available Presence	# New Outlets with Brand A Presence	Brand A % coverage of new outlets	# of Outlets with Brand A Presence and rented Prominence
Hypermarkets								
– in-store								
– online								
Supermarkets								
– in-store								
– online								
Discounters								
– in-store								
– online								
Club stores								
– in-store								
– online								
Convenience stores								
– in-store								
– online								
Specialist pet retailers								
– in-store								
– online								
Direct-to-consumer websites								
Online-only market places								
Veterinarians								
Any other								
Total all options								

balance to avoid holding on to the past for too long (e.g., investing in lots of factories to build petrol/gas-powered cars) and investing in the future too heavily and/or too early (e.g., investing heavily in R&D on autonomous cars). The aim is to continually stay relevant to as many category buyers as possible.

You need to plan because there is usually a time lag between identifying the need for a new Portfolio addition and being able to deliver the new product or service. For example, there are more older dogs due to an increase in dog life expectancy (Grimm 2015). Recognising this trend as a dog food manufacturer can lead to more investment in foods that can improve the quality of life for older dogs; however, it takes time to test ingredients, create a product and build the manufacturing capacity to deliver this as a buyable option.

As marketers, we often jump too fast and too furiously on the 'we need something new' bandwagon. Before we shift investment from marketing we have (the safe bet) to speculate on 'something new' (the long shot), it is prudent to have Portfolio effectiveness metrics in place to assess the wisdom of this decision. This checks any decisions to extend the Portfolio by taking into account potential downsides such as potential harm to the core product/service, as well as the often widely touted potential upsides.

If you have multiple brands in the same category, then Portfolio mapping needs to take place across all brands to avoid wasting company resources competing unnecessarily with the brand's stablemates, particularly in small parts of the market. It also ensures that the company can assess which of the total Portfolio on offer is best placed to offer any new line extension.

Portfolio management: Suggested tracking metrics

There are two key aspects to monitor for Portfolio management: Portfolio size and Portfolio contribution.

Portfolio size

While marketers get to influence the number of items in a brand's Portfolio, each option comes with additional costs; therefore, a common question is, *Do we have too many or too few options?* We know that the typically larger the brand share, the wider the Portfolio (Tanusondjaja et al. 2018a), and while does not mean that adding to the Portfolio will automatically lead to growth, it does give us a way to see if your Portfolio size in normal. If you are the largest brand in a category, you should have the largest number or Stock Keeping Units (SKU), and if you are the smallest, the fewest number.

If you are a large brand with relatively few options available to buy, you may identify some missing growth opportunities to capitalise upon. However, if you are a small brand with many, many Portfolio options, you probably have some inefficiencies that, if addressed, could lead to better resource allocation.

The key is to calculate Portfolio size from a customer perspective, which is how many different options can customers buy. Rather than just take the company's list, which may include options that are obsolete or unavailable, include each variant/option, as each of these options costs the company in terms of resources in development and maintenance, and the category buyer in search/decision costs. Tracking how this evolves over time is critical to avoid fragmentation and adding unnecessary and unhelpful complexity.

- Metric to track: *Number of products sold, relative to competitors and market share.*

Portfolio contribution

Most brands have a core product/service that is responsible for a large proportion of the brand's sales. In packaged goods, benchmarking studies have shown that one SKU often contributes 50% of the brand's penetration and 40% of the brand's sales (Tanusondjaja et al. 2018b).

In an Ehrenberg-Bass Institute survey of over 600 business-to-business (B2B) marketers across a range of industries, 30% could not estimate the sales contribution of their biggest product. This 'don't know' figure was lower in technology industries, software (13%) and hardware (15%) and higher in government/not for profits (66%), large durables (56%) and commodities (43%). Of those that could provide an estimate, this was 53%, but this figure was very similar for companies with six to ten products and companies with over 50 products (Romaniuk and Vaughan 2023).

This suggests that this could be a guesstimate rather than based on fact, so encouraging more people to calculate this figure would help improve Portfolio knowledge. Alternatively, if this is a real figure, there are many B2B companies with many products that contribute little to the bottom line, and so many opportunities exist to get more efficient product Portfolios. If you have 50 products and one of those products is responsible for 53% of sales, then there must be some of the 49 remaining products that contribute very little to the bottom line.

This information can then inform the case for change when new introductions are suggested that might challenge the core for resources— the brand exists because of its core product/service and this part of the Portfolio needs to be protected.

- Metric: *% contribution of each product sold to sales.*
- Metric: *% contribution of each product sold to brand penetration.*

Addressing Portfolio gaps

If the role of Portfolio is to cover the market (price points, key occasions etc), how can we uncover gaps in coverage?

In Chapter 1 we talked about the Duplication of Purchase law, which was developed through analysis into patterns of how category buyers buy across brands. You can conduct this same analysis using key product attributes (e.g., price points) to understand market structure. This can uncover gaps that can be filled by new line extensions. While for many marketers this can be seen as mundane, adding a pack size to be able to be listed at Costco or adding a multipack to address the needs of an online channel might end up being the 'innovation' of the year!

What to monitor

In the first instance, this analysis is a strategic piece, taking stock of where you are now and making the changes needed to get the brand into the best position for the future. There is only the need to repeat this analysis every two or three years to identify any new emerging opportunities. Some of the data for this analysis can be collected via a well-designed survey if recorded data is not easily available.

Prominence

The third pillar of Physical Availability is Prominence, which covers the tactics to help the brand stand out in sales environments. While many sales environments also have competitors present, all sales environments, even the ones you own, have environmental clutter that can interfere with the buyer easily finding the option they want to buy. Therefore, Prominence matters, even if you are the only brand being sold in the channel.

You can *own* or *rent* Prominence:

- *Owned Prominence* – This happens through the building of shopping Distinctive Assets, which are branding devices that can be used in sales environments (Nenycz-Thiel and Romaniuk 2021). The company owns and can control this investment, and these assets can be used in the long term, provided investments are made wisely.

- *Rented Prominence* – This is when you pay for better real estate within a shopping environment; for example, to be on the first online page, to be top search result, or to place an end cap with the product at the end of an aisle, or use front-of-store placement so even shoppers who did not go down the category aisle can see the brand.

Shopping Distinctive Assets

Distinctive Assets are the non-brand name elements that can trigger the brand in the minds of category buyers (Romaniuk 2018a). Shopping Distinctive Assets are a sub-set of the visual assets that can be used in sales environments to help shoppers easily locate the brand in-store, online or on-phone.

Although typically thought of in the context of consumer-packaged goods, all categories, including services and durables, can have shopping Distinctive Assets (see Table 14.3). Logos on websites, thumbnail images on apps and mobile-enabled sites, and signage on streets are all opportunities for any brand that wants to build Prominence among competitor and environmental clutter.

Once developed, shopping Distinctive Assets need consistent use to avoid memory decay. Therefore, these assets should be used consistently and boldly on websites, packs, apps, stores—everywhere with valuable Presence investments that you want the category buyer to notice.

Table 14.3: Three examples of shopping Distinctive Assets across asset types

Packaged goods	Services	Durables
Logos	Logos	Logos
Pack shape	Membership/credit card	Product shape
Pack closure	colour and/or images	Product colours
Images on pack	Staff uniforms	Outer packaging
Face on pack	Store signage and livery	Specialist retail store or staff
Pack style	Mobile apps	livery
Colours		

Renting Prominence

Many channels offer options where brands pay more to get better real estate, such as the following:

- Supermarkets offer front and back endcaps or off locations in a totally different part of the store (e.g., events, front of the store).
- Online search engines offer paid search to increase the odds of coming up at the top of the search site, or you can pay to be in the advertising at the top of the search page before organic search options.
- Social media sites offer options for e-commerce enabled advertisements to be served earlier when someone scrolls or to be placed in better locations on the site.
- Online retailers offer the ability to be on the first page of the category options.

We call this *renting* Prominence because most sales effects are a temporary lift over the duration of the intervention, with sales reverting to normal once you stop paying the rent, and next month another brand can rent the same advantage. Not all rental forms of Prominence are equal; for example, research into endcaps shows that the back of the store location is more effective in driving sales from the main shelf than the front of the store location, because the back of the store endcaps act as a reminder that the category exists and the buyer can more easily change their path to go to the category (Tan et al. 2018).

Renting Prominence should never replace building the brand's owned Prominence. Having strong Distinctive Assets can also help you gain more from some rental tactics by drawing more category buyer attention due to their familiarity with the assets. Rental tactics that use Distinctive Assets can also reinforce the brand's visual identity and avert decay, which provides benefits after you have stopped paying the rent.

However, we should make informed decisions about what to rent and what rental Prominence properties are worth. Such knowledge will come from research and experimentation as well as learning from past investments.

Prominence management: Suggested tracking metrics

Distinctive Assets

To identify the options for the brand to develop shopping Distinctive Assets, we recommend a specialist piece of research outside of the tracker. However, once identified, these assets can be included in the subset of Distinctive Assets tracked on an annual or two-yearly basis. The recommended metrics are Fame and Uniqueness of these assets (as per Romaniuk 2018a):

- *Fame* = % of category buyers that link the brand to the asset, without prompting for the brand
- *Uniqueness* = % of linkages the asset gets that are for the brand (versus competitors).

For both metrics we want the results to be as close to 100% as possible. See Romaniuk (2021d) and Nenycz-Thiel and Romaniuk (2021) for more detail on tactics to build shopping Distinctive Assets.

Rented Prominence

There are many different rented Prominence tactics within and across categories. At the most basic level we recommend metric tracking the number of outlets where Presence is boosted with rented Prominence. This creates a starting point for you to check the effectiveness of specific types of rented Prominence (off locations, paid search etc).

This can be done by adding a column to Table 14.2 (see column 9) to track number of outlets with Brand A Presence and rented Prominence.

Can we ask category buyers what they think?

Sometimes trackers include aspects of Physical Availability in brand attribute lists to get category buyer perceptions about brands. Table 14.4 lists some examples.

Table 14.4: Types of Physical Availability attributes

Presence	Portfolio	Prominence
Has convenient locations Is available everywhere Not available everywhere (exclusive distribution) Provides great online services	Has a variety of flavours Has a wide range of products/services Has premium options Has cheaper options Has (insert specialist ingredient/flavour)	Has packaging that stands out on shelf Has distinctive packaging Is a brand that's easy to find Has appealing packaging

There are two problems with tracking Physical Availability as attributes. First, as with heuristics, the 'correct' answers can change with the time and place of retrieval. *Which* brands meet the criteria of *conveniently located* is dependent on where someone is physically located. For example, options that fit *a conveniently located place for lunch* vary substantively whether someone is at home or at the office.

Even if it is modified for the location, what is *convenient at lunchtime* for one person when in the office is going to be different from what is convenient for another person when in their office, even if they are in the same city. Therefore, the responses to these attributes are of very little value.

The second issue is the accuracy of response. Inherent in asking the question is the assumption that people will notice and process the results of good Physical Availability, so if they say it is good, it really is good, and if they identify a problem, it really is a problem. How valid is that assumption—do people really need to notice the size of a brand's Portfolio to be able to judge if a brand has 'a wide range of options'? Or do people really need to know where a brand is sold to know if it is 'available in a wide range of locations'? If the answers do not resemble reality, then we do not know what we are measuring and the results are of little value.

To illustrate, we tested if people could correctly identify the retailers where different fitness trackers were sold. All respondents had either bought a fitness tracker in the last 12 months or had a non-zero probability of buying a fitness tracker in the next 12 months. Across four brands in the category (Fitbit, Garmin, Goji and Apple iWatch), the results show people underestimated the retailers where they were available (see Table 14.5). On average 31% correctly identified a retailer as a sales channel, 69% did not know the retailer sold the brand, and in about one in ten cases, people incorrectly named a retailer. Incorrect retailer linkage is more common for Goji, which is not as widely distributed as the other brands.

The results across retailers show that category buyers generally underestimate Presence and make assumptions about a brand's availability in common channels. Without accurate knowledge of Presence, category buyers are unlikely to be able to give an accurate answer to whether the brand is *widely available* or *convenient to buy*.

Table 14.5: Results for retailer Presence accuracy test in fitness trackers, United Kingdom (n=790)

Averages across 22 retailers	Fitbit	Garmin	Goji	Apple iWatch	Average
Recognition of correct retailer	24	30	38	34	31
Did not know a retailer where the brand is stocked	79	67	62	69	69
Claimed a retailer incorrectly stocked the brand	12	11	27	5	13
Results for specific retailers					
Amazon.co.uk	63	76	62*	74	69
Argos	67	74	51	60	63
Curry's	68	77	38	56	60
John Lewis	42	50	26	43	40
Tesco	32	34	21	13	25

*Shaded cells represent retailers where the brand is not available, so an incorrect response.

In general, if you test Physical Availability characteristics as attributes, the influences on brand responses (discussed in Chapter 3 and 4) overwhelm any assessment of specific brands, which makes the results difficult to interpret or action.

For example, attributes such as *stands out on shelf* or *easy to find on shelf* pop up in trackers as an attempt to capture the brand's Prominence. It turns out that responses to these attributes follow the same patterns as other attributes, which means buyers generally think their brand stands out more than non-buyers think the brand they don't buy stands out! This makes it difficult to conclude that the attribute responses are an objective assessment of any brand's ability to stand out on shelf.

Table 14.6 shows an example from a pet food category in Europe, which shows an average of around three times higher response levels from brand buyers and a high correlation with brand penetration.

Table 14.6: Responses to attribute of a brand that stands out on shelf in pet food category, Europe (2020)

	% buyers	% responses	% buyer responses	% non-buyer responses
Brand 1	44	43	66	25
Brand 2	44	41	56	29
Brand 3	31	35	55	26
Brand 4	29	29	52	20
Brand 5	23	23	47	15
Brand 6	19	19	40	15
Brand 7	20	18	48	11
Brand 8	15	18	46	13
Brand 9	11	13	36	10
Brand 10	10	8	39	5
Average	**25**	**25**	**49**	**17**
Correlation with buying		**98%**	**92%**	**94%**

Therefore, converting the pillars of Physical Availability into attributes produces little insight into a brand's Physical Availability and adds little value to a brand tracker.

Chapter summary

This chapter covers some initial tracking metrics to monitor your Physical Availability investments and future-proof your brand in the three areas of Presence, Portfolio and Prominence.

The key message we want to embed here is that *you* should keep track of your Physical Availability investments instead of solely relying on the third-party data providers. Such practice gives you control over what you inspect for better performance and faster access, and allows you to work with your data provider in your category on better coverage in the future.

While most data to monitor Physical Availability will come from outside of the survey, the CBM tracker can play a supporting role. Some of the data from the CBM tracker will be helpful in informing questions to ask in areas of Portfolio (e.g., CEP data) or Presence (e.g., brand buying data). Finally, if we see deviations from expected patterns or weaknesses on our brands in the tracker, we should always ask: what role could Physical Availably play in explaining and fixing those deficits?

A Final Note

Thank you for taking the time to read this book. It was a challenging one to write because I had to go back to where I started my branding research career, and review over a decade of papers and theses, as well as practical experience with brand tracking instruments to pull this one together. Some research needed updating, which meant doing quite a few replications to include in the book, alongside the original studies. That these mostly replicated past results is reassuring about the robustness of the knowledge, and the small parts that didn't are fuel for my future curiosity.

COVID also got in the way with other demands on my time, pandemic malaise and burnout all hitting, so in my mind this book is about two years late—but hopefully better late than never! I just kept thinking about the Chinese proverb, *The best time to plant a tree is 20 years ago, the second best time is now.* For me it became *The best time to finish writing a book is 2 years ago, the second best time is now!* That thought kept me going through this long-term project.

It was fun to revisit some of the more nerdy analysis I have undertaken looking at the underlying patterns in how people respond to brand health questions. It also reignited my passion to do more, as there is still so much to learn.

Please let me know what questions you still have after reading this book, and I can see if I can tackle them in the next round of research. Don't forget to check out jenni.romaniuk.com for sample questionnaires and other bits and pieces to help you use the information in this book.

Finally, to reiterate my request at the start of the book, if you do want to support research in the area and have data available, please do get in touch.

Cheers, Jenni

REFERENCE LIST

Aaker, D. A. and G. Shansby (1982). Positioning your product. *Business Horizons*, **25**: 56–62.

Aaker, J. L. (1997). Dimensions of brand personality. *Journal of Marketing Research*, **34**(August): 347–356.

Ajzen, I. (1991). The theory of planned behavior. *Organizational Behavior and Human Decision Processes*, **50**(2): 179–211.

Ambler, T. (2003). *Marketing and the Bottom Line*. London, United Kingdom, Pearson Publication.

Anderson, J. R. and G. H. Bower (1973). *Human Associative Memory*. Washington, DC, Hemisphere Publishing Corporation.

Anderson, J. R. and G. H. Bower (1979). *Human Associative Memory*. Hillsdale, NJ, Lawrence Erlbaum.

Anesbury, Z., M. Nenycz-Thiel, J. Dawes and R. Kennedy (2016). How do shoppers behave online? An observational study of online grocery shopping. *Journal of Consumer Behaviour*, **15**(3): 261–270.

Anesbury, Z., M. Winchester and R. Kennedy (2017). Brand user profiles seldom change and seldom differ. *Marketing Letters*, **28**(4): 523–535.

Anesbury, Z. W., D. Bennett and R. Kennedy (2021). How persistent are duplication of purchase partitions? *Journal of Consumer Behaviour*, **21**(1): 137–152.

Assael, H. and G. S. Day (1968). Attitudes and awareness as predictors of market share. *Journal of Advertising Research*, **8**(4): 3–10.

Avis, M. (2012). Brand personality factor based models: A critical review. *Australasian Marketing Journal*, **20**(1): 89–96.

Avis, M. and R. Aitken (2015). Intertwined: Brand personification, brand personality and brand relationships in historical perspective. *Journal of Historical Research in Marketing*, **7**(2).

Avis, M., R. Aitken and S. Ferguson (2012). Brand relationship and personality theory metaphor or consumer perceptual reality? *Marketing Theory*, **12**(3): 311–331.

Axelrod, J. N. (1968). Attitude measures that predict purchase. *Journal of Advertising Research*, **8**(1): 3–17.

Banelis, M., E. Riebe and C. Rungie (2013). Empirical evidence of repertoire size. *Australasian Marketing Journal*, **21**(1): 59–65.

Barnard, N. R. and A. Ehrenberg (1990). Robust measures of consumer brand beliefs. *Journal of Marketing Research*, **27**(4): 477–484.

Barsalou, L. W. (1983). Ad hoc categories. *Memory & Cognition*, **11**(No. 3): 211–227.

Batra, R., A. Ahuvia and R. Bagozzi (2012). Brand love. *Journal of Marketing*, **76**(2): 1–16.

Beckwith, N. E. and D. R. Lehmann (1975). The importance of halo effects in multi-attribute attitude models. *Journal of Marketing Research*, **12**(3): 265–275.

Bird, M., C. Channon and A. S. C. Ehrenberg (1970). Brand image and brand usage. *Journal of Marketing Research*, **7**(3): 307–314.

Brennan, M. (2004). The Juster Purchase Probability Scale: A bibliography. *Marketing Bulletin*, **15**(May).

Brooks Jr., R. C. (1957). Word of mouth advertising in selling new products. *Journal of Marketing*, **22**(2): 54–161.

Colicev, A., A. Malshe, K. Pauwels and P. O'Connor (2018). Improving consumer mindset metrics and shareholder value through social media: The different roles of owned and earned media. *Journal of Marketing*, **82**(1): 37–56.

Collins, A. M. and E. F. Loftus (1975). A spreading activation theory of semantic processing. *Psychological Review*, **82**(6): 407–428.

Dall'Olmo Riley, F., A. Ehrenberg, S. B. Castleberry, T. P. Barwise and N. R. Barnard (1997). The variability of attitudinal repeat-rates. *International Journal of Research in Marketing*, **14**(5): 437–450.

Dawes, J. (2020). The natural monopoly effect in brand purchasing: Do big brands really appeal to lighter category buyers? *Australasian Marketing Journal*, **28**(2): 90–99.

Dawes, J., C. Graham, G. Trinh and B. Sharp (2022). The unbearable lightness of buying. *Journal of Marketing Management*, **38**(7–8): 683–708.

Dawes, J., J. Romaniuk and A. Mansfield (2009). Generalized pattern in competition among tourism destinations. *International Journal of Culture, Tourism and Hospitality Research*, **3**(1): 33–53.

Day, G. S. (1970). *Buyer Attitudes and Brand Choice*. New York, The Free Press.

Day, G. S. and R. W. Pratt (1971). Stability of appliance brand awareness. *Journal of Marketing Research*, **8**(February): 85–89.

Desai, K. K. and W. D. Hoyer (2000). Descriptive characteristics of memory-based consideration sets: Influence of usage occasion frequency and usage location frequency. *Journal of Consumer Research*, **27**(3): 309–323.

Dick, A. S. and K. Basu (1994). Customer loyalty: Toward an integrated conceptual framework. *Journal of the Academy of Marketing Science*, **22**(No. 2): 99–113.

Dickson, P. R. and A. G. Sawyer (1990). The price knowledge and search of supermarket shoppers. *Journal of Marketing*, **54**(3): 42–53.

Driesener, C. and J. Romaniuk (2006). Comparing methods of brand image measurement. *International Journal of Market Research*, **48**(6): 681–698.

Dunn, S., C. Graham, M. Nenycz-Thiel and A. Tanusondjaja (2021). Investigating undercurrents of stationarity and growth with long-term panel data. *International Journal of Market Research*, **63**(6): 786–809.

Dwivedi, A., L. W. Johnson, D. C. Wilkie and L. De Araujo-Gil (2018). Consumer emotional brand attachment with social media brands and social media brand equity. *European Journal of Marketing*, **53**(6): 1176–1204.

East, R., K. Hammond and W. Lomax (2008). Measuring the impact of positive and negative word of mouth on brand purchase probability. *International Journal of Research in Marketing*, **25**(3): 215–224.

East, R., K. Hammond and M. Wright (2007). The relative incidence of positive and negative word of mouth: A multi-category study. *International Journal of Research in Marketing*, **24**(2): 175–184.

East, R., J. Romaniuk and W. Lomax (2011). The NPS and the ACSI: A critique and an alternative metric. *International Journal of Market Research*, **53**(3): 15.

East, R., M. Uncles, J. Romaniuk and W. Lomax (2017). Social amplification: A mechanism in the spread of brand usage. *Australasian Marketing Journal*, **25**(1): 20–25.

East, R., M. Uncles, J. Romaniuk and F. D. O. Riley (2015). Factors associated with the production of word of mouth. *International Journal of Market Research*, **57**(3): 439–458.

Ehrenberg, A., G. Goodhardt and T. P. Barwise (1990). Double Jeopardy revisited. *Journal of Marketing*, **54**(3): 82–91.

Ehrenberg, A. S. C. (1959). The pattern of consumer purchases. *Applied Statistics*, **8**(1): 26–41.

Engagement Labs (2021). Word of mouth remains a juggernaut: A 15-year WOM measurement journey. Available at https://blog.engagementlabs.com/word-of-mouth-remains-a-juggernaut-a-15-year-wom-measurement-journey

Fetscherin, M. (2019). The five types of brand hate: How they affect consumer behavior. *Journal of Business Research*, **101**: 116–127.

Fishbein, M. and I. Ajzen (1975). *Belief, Attitude, Intention and Behaviour: An Introduction to Theory and Research*. Reading, MA, Addison-Wesley Publishing Company.

Foroudi, P., Z. Jin, S. Gupta, M. M. Foroudi and P. J. Kitchen (2018). Perceptional components of brand equity: Configuring the symmetrical and asymmetrical paths to brand loyalty and brand purchase intention. *Journal of Business Research*, **89**: 462–474.

Fortenberry, J. L. and P. J. McGoldrick (2020). Do billboard advertisements drive customer retention?: Expanding the 'AIDA' model to 'AIDAR'. *Journal of Advertising Research*, **60**(2): 135–147.

Fournier, S. (1998). Consumers and their brands: Developing relationship theory in consumer research. *Journal of Consumer Research*, **24**(4): 343–353.

Gardner, B. B. and S. J. Levy (1955). The product and the brand. *Harvard Business Review*, **33**(2): 33–39.

Goodhardt, G. J. and A. Ehrenberg (1969). Duplication of viewing between and within channels. *Journal of Marketing Research*, **6**(2): 169–178.

Goodhardt, G. J., A. Ehrenberg and C. Chatfield (1984). The Dirichlet: A comprehensive model of buying behaviour. *Journal of the Royal Statistical Society*, **147**(5): 621–643.

Graham, C. and R. Kennedy (2021). Quantifying the target market for advertisers. *Journal of Consumer Behaviour*, **21**(1): 33–48.

Grasby, A., A. Corsi, J. Dawes, C. Driesener and B. Sharp (2022). How loyalty extends across product categories. *Journal of Consumer Behaviour*, **21**(1): 153–163.

Grimm, D. (2015). Feature: A dog that lives 300 years? Solving the mysteries of aging in our pets. Available at https://www.science.org/content/article/feature-dog-lives-300-years-solving-mysteries-aging-our-pets.

Gruber, A. (1969). Top-of-mind awareness and share of families: An observation. *Journal of Marketing Research*, **6**(May): 227–231.

Han, J. A., E. M. Feit and S. Srinivasan (2020). Can negative buzz increase awareness and purchase intent? *Marketing Letters*, **31**(1): 89–104.

Harrison, F. (2013). Digging deeper down into the empirical generalization of brand recall. *Journal of Advertising Research*, **53**(2): 181–185.

Hartnett, N., A. Gelzinis, V. Beal, R. Kennedy and B. Sharp (2021). When brands go dark: Examining sales trends when brands stop broad-reach advertising for long periods. *Journal of Advertising Research*, **61**(3): 247–259.

Hasher, L. and R. T. Zacks (1984). Automatic processing of fundamental information: The case of frequency of occurrence. *American Psychologist*, **39**(12): 1372–1388.

Heath, R. (2000). Low involvement processing: A new model of brands and advertising. *International Journal of Advertising*, **19**(3): 287–298.

Hofmann, J., O. Schnittka, M. Johnen and P. Kottemann (2021). Talent or popularity: What drives market value and brand image for human brands? *Journal of Business Research*, **124**: 748–758.

Hogan, S. (2015). *Are You Keeping Track of Your Light Buyers? Understanding and Measuring Light Buyer Brand Equity.* Ehrenberg-Bass Institute, University of South Australia.

Holden, S. J. and R. J. Lutz (1992). Ask not what the brand can evoke: Ask what can evoke the brand? *Advances in Consumer Research*, **19**(1): 101–107.

Holden, S. J. S. (1993). Understanding brand awareness: Let me give you a c(l)ue! *Advances in Consumer Research*, **20**(1): 383–388.

Howard, J. A. and J. N. Sheth (1969). *The Theory of Buyer Behavior.* New York, John & Wiley Sons, Inc.

Hoyer, W. D. and S. P. Brown (1990). Effects of brand awareness on choice for a common, repeat-purchase product. *Journal of Consumer Research*, **17**(2): 141–148.

Joyce, T. (1963). Techniques of brand image measurement. New developments in research. London, United Kingdom, *Market Research Society*: 45–63.

Juster, F. T. (1966). Consumer buying intentions and purchase probability: An experiment in survey design. *Journal of American Statistical Association*, **61**(315): 658–696.

Kahneman, D., P. Slovic and A. Tversky, Eds. (1982). *Judgment Under Uncertainty: Heuristics and Biases.* Cambridge University Press.

Kalwani, M. U. and A. J. Silk (1982). On the reliability and predictive validity of purchase intention measures. *Marketing Science*, **1**(3): 243–286.

Lam, D. and B. Ozorio (2013). Duplication of purchase law in the gaming entertainment industry: A transnational investigation. *International Journal of Hospitality Management*, **33**: 203–207.

LaPiere, R. (1934). Attitudes vs actions. *Social Forces*, **13**(2): 7.

Laurent, G., J.-N. Kapferer and F. Roussel (1995). The underlying structure of brand awareness scores. *Marketing Science*, **14**(No. 3, Part 2): G170–G179.

Levitt, T. (1980). Marketing success through differentiation: Of anything. *Harvard Business Review* (January–February): 83–91.

Likert, R. (1932). A technique for the emasurement of attitudes. *Archives of Psychology*, **140**: 44–53.

Louviere, J. J. and G. G. Woodworth (1991). Best-worst scaling: A model for the largest difference judgments. University of Alberta: Working Paper.

Ludwichowska, G. (2013). Can we fix errors in self-reported buying frequencies?, University of South Australia.

Ludwichowska, G., J. Romaniuk and M. Nenycz-Thiel (2017). Systematic response errors in self-reported category buying frequencies. *European Journal of Marketing*, **51**(7/8): 1440–1459.

Lynn, M. (2013). Lessons from duplication of purchase data. *Cornell Hospitality Report*, **13**(3): 4–16.

Macdonald, E. and B. Sharp (2000). Brand awareness effects on consumer decision making for a common, repeat purchase product: A replication. *Journal of Business Research*, **48**(1): 5–15.

Macdonald, E. and B. Sharp (2003). Management perceptions of the the importance of brand awareness as an indicator of advertising effectiveness. *Marketing Bulletin*, **14**: article 2.

Mangold, W. G., F. Miller and G. R. Brockway (1999). Word-of-mouth communication in the service marketplace. *Journal of Services Marketing*, **13**(1): 73–89.

McDonald, C. and A. Ehrenberg (2003). What happens when brands gain or lose share? Customer acquisition or increased loyalty? *Report 31 for Corporate Sponsors*. Adelaide, Ehrenberg-Bass Institute for Marketing Science: 1–2.

Morwitz, V. G., J. H. Steckel and A. Gupta (2007). When do purchase intentions predict sales? *International Journal of Forecasting*, **23**(3): 347–364.

Nelson-Field, K., E. Riebe and B. Sharp (2012). What's not to "like?: Can a Facebook fan base give a brand the advertising reach it needs? *Journal of Advertising Research*, **2**: 262–269.

Nenycz-Thiel, M. (2010). Understanding consumer knowledge about private labels. A study of brand perception and rejection. PhD thesis, University of South Australia.

Nenycz-Thiel, M., V. Beal, G. Ludwichowska and J. Romaniuk (2013). Investigating the accuracy of self-reports of brand usage behavior. *Journal of Business Research*, **66**(2): 224–232.

Nenycz-Thiel, M., J. Dawes and J. Romaniuk (2018). Modeling brand market share change in emerging markets. *International Marketing Review*, **35**(5): 785–805.

Nenycz-Thiel, M. and J. Romaniuk (2021). Building physical availability: Prominence and portfolio. *How Brands Grow: Part 2*. J. Butler. Victoria, Australia, Oxford University Press: 159–172.

Nenycz-Thiel, M., J. Romaniuk and B. Sharp (2021). Building physical availability: Presence. *How Brands Grow: Part 2*. J. Butler. Victoria, Australia, Oxford University Press: 140–158.

Ngo, L. V., G. Gregory, R. Miller and L. Lu (2021). Understanding the role of brand salience in brand choice decisions in the charity sector. *Australasian Marketing Journal*, **29**(1): 1–13.

Page, B., A. Barker, and J. Romaniuk (2023). Wider or deeper: An examination of the category entry points for big brands, Ehrenberg-Bass Institute, White Paper.

Paivio, A. and K. Csapo (1973). Picture superiority in free recall: Imagery or dual coding? *Cognitive Psychology*, **5**(2): 176–206.

Patrick, S., J. Romaniuk, V. Beal and B. Sharp (2018). Comparing the customer profiles of rival luxury brands. *Report 81 for Corporate Sponsors*. Adelaide, Ehrenberg-Bass Institute for Marketing Science.

Ratneshwar, S. and A. D. Shocker (1991). Substitution in use and the role of usage context in product category structures. *Journal of Marketing Research*, **28**(3): 281–295.

Riebe, E., M. Wright, P. Stern and B. Sharp (2014). How to grow a brand: Retain or acquire customers? *Journal of Business Research*, **67**(5): 990–997.

Ries, A. and J. Trout (1981). *Positioning: The Battle for Your Mind*. New York, McGrawHill.

Romaniuk, J. (2000). Brand image and loyalty. PhD Dissertation, University of South Australia.

Romaniuk, J. (2001). Brand positioning in financial services: A longitudinal test to find the best brand position. *Journal of Financial Services Marketing*, **6**(2): 111–121.

Romaniuk, J. (2003). Brand attributes: 'Distribution outlets' in the mind. *Journal of Marketing Communications*, **9**(June): 73–92.

Romaniuk, J. (2006). Comparing prompted and unprompted methods for measuring consumer brand associations. *Journal of Targeting, Measurement and Analysis for Marketing*, **15**(1): 3–11.

Romaniuk, J. (2008). Comparing methods of measuring brand personality traits. *The Journal of Marketing Theory and Practice*, **16**(2): 153–161.

Romaniuk, J. (2013). Modeling mental market share. *Journal of Business Research*, **66**(2): 188–195.

Romaniuk, J. (2018a). *Building Distinctive Brand Assets*. South Melbourne, Victoria, Oxford University Press.

Romaniuk, J. (2018b). Creating a distinctive asset management system. *Building Distinctive Brand Assets*. J. Romaniuk. South Melbourne, Victoria, Oxford University Press: 163–170.

Romaniuk, J. (2018c). Setting a distinctive asset-building strategy. *Building Distinctive Brand Assets*. J. Romaniuk. South Melbourne, Victoria, Oxford University Press: 97–107.

Romaniuk, J. (2021a). Building mental availability. *How Brands Grow: Part 2*. J. Butler. Victoria, Australia, Oxford University Press: 61–84.

Romaniuk, J. (2021b). Getting down to business-to-business markets. *How Brands Grow: Part 2*. J. Butler. Victoria, Australia, Oxford University Press: 190–211.

Romaniuk, J. (2021c). How do business-to-business (B2B) brands compete? An application of the duplication of purchase law. Ehrenberg-Bass Institute for Marketing Science: 1–8.

Romaniuk, J. (2021d). Leveraging distinctive assets. *How Brands Grow: Part 2*. J. Butler. Victoria, Australia, Oxford University Press: 85–103.

Romaniuk, J. (2022). Category entry points in a B2B world: Linking buying situations to brand sales. Ehrenberg-Bass Institute for Marketing Science: 1–33.

Romaniuk, J., S. Bogomolova and F. Dall'Olmo Riley (2012). Brand image and brand usage: Is a forty-year-old empirical generalization still useful? *Journal of Advertising Research*, **52**(2): 243–251.

Romaniuk, J., J. Dawes and M. Nenycz-Thiel (2014). Generalizations regarding the growth and decline of manufacturer and store brands. *Journal of Retailing and Consumer Services*, **21**(5): 725–734.

Romaniuk, J. and R. East (2016). Word-of-mouth facts worth talking about. *How Brands Grow: Part 2*. J. Romaniuk and B. Sharp. Melbourne, Oxford University Press: 125–144.

Romaniuk, J., R. East and C. Nguyen (2010). The accuracy of self-reported probabilities of giving recommendations. *International Journal of Market Research*, **53**(4): 507–521.

Romaniuk, J. and A. Ehrenberg (2012). Do brands lack personality? *Marketing Theory: An International Review*, **12**(3): 333–339.

Romaniuk, J. and A. Huang (2019). Understanding consumer perceptions of luxury brands. *International Journal of Market Research*, **62**(5): 546–560.

Romaniuk, J., M. Nenycz-Thiel and O. Truong (2012). Do consumers reject brands? Which, where and how often. Report 61 for Corporate Sponsors. Adelaide, Ehrenberg-Bass Institute for Marketing Science.

Romaniuk, J. and E. Nicholls (2006). Evaluating advertising effects on brand perceptions: Incorporating prior knowledge. *International Journal of Market Research*, **48**(2): 179–192.

Romaniuk, J. and B. Sharp (2000). Using known patterns in image data to determine brand positioning. *International Journal of Market Research*, **42**(2): 219–230.

Romaniuk, J. and B. Sharp (2003a). Brand salience and customer defection in subscription markets. *Journal of Marketing Management*, **19**: 25–44.

Romaniuk, J. and B. Sharp (2003b). Measuring brand perceptions: Testing quantity and quality. *Journal of Targeting, Measurement and Analysis for Marketing*, **11**(3): 218–229.

Romaniuk, J. and B. Sharp (2004). Conceptualizing and measuring brand salience. *Marketing Theory*, **4**(4): 327–342.

Romaniuk, J. and B. Sharp (2016). And finally, a bit of luxury. *How Brands Grow: Part 2*. J. Romaniuk and B. Sharp. Melbourne, Oxford University Press: 203–221.

Romaniuk, J. and B. Sharp (2021). *How Brands Grow: Part 2*. Victoria, Australia, Oxford University Press.

Romaniuk, J., B. Sharp, S. Paech and C. Driesener (2004). Brand and advertising awareness: A replication and extension of a known empirical generalisation. *Australasian Marketing Journal*, **12**(3): 70–80.

Romaniuk, J. and K. Vaughan (2023). Physical availability for B2B marketers. Adelaide, South Australia, Ehrenberg-Bass Institute Working Paper: 1–10.

Rosch, E. and C. B. Mervis (1975). Family resemblances: Studies in the internal structure of categories. *Cognitive Psychology*, **7**: 573–605.

Rungie, C., G. Laurent, F. Dall'Olmo Riley, D. G. Morrison and T. Roy (2005). Measuring and modeling the (limited) reliability of free choice attitude questions. *International Journal of Research in Marketing*, **22**(3): 309–318.

Schoenmueller, V., O. Netzer and F. Stahl (2020). The polarity of online reviews: Prevalence, drivers and implications. *Journal of Marketing Research*, **57**(5): 853–877.

Sharp, A. (2002). Searching for boundary conditions for an empirical generalisation concerning the temporal stability of individual's perceptual responses. PhD Doctor of Philosophy, University of South Australia.

Sharp, B. (2010). *How Brands Grow*. Melbourne, Oxford University Press.

Sharp, B. (2017). *Marketing: Theory, Evidence, Practice*. Melbourne, Oxford University Press.

Sharp, B. and J. Romaniuk (2016). Where new customers come from. *How Brands Grow: Part 2*. J. Romaniuk and B. Sharp. Melbourne, Oxford University Presss: 43–61.

Sharp, B. and J. Romaniuk (2021a). How brands grow. *How Brands Grow: Part 2*. Victoria, Australia, Oxford University Press: 1–20.

Sharp, B. and J. Romaniuk (2021b). Target the (whole) market. *How Brands Grow: Part 2*. Victoria, Australia, Oxford University Press: 22–39.

Simmonds, L., S. Bellman, R. Kennedy, M. Nenycz-Thiel and S. Bogomolova (2020). Moderating effects of prior brand usage on visual attention to video advertising and recall: An eye-tracking investigation. *Journal of Business Research*, **111**: 241–248.

Singh, J., A. Ehrenberg and G. Goodhardt (2008). Measuring customer loyalty to product variants. *International Journal of Market Research*, **50**(4): 513–532.

Sirgy, M. J. (1985). Using self-congruity and ideal congruity to predict purchase motivation. *Journal of Business Research*, **13**: 195–206.

Stern, P. and A. Ehrenberg (2002). Expectations and reality for doctor's prescribing behaviour: How do prescribing drugs grow? Report 30 for Corporate Sponsors. Adelaide, Ehrenberg-Bass Institute for Marketing Science: 1–2.

Stocchi, L., E. Kemps and Z. Anesbury (2021). The effect of mental availability on snack food choices. *Journal of Retailing and Consumer Services*, **60**.

Surowiecki, J. (2004). *The Wisdom of Crowds: Why the Many Are Smarter Than the Few and How Collective Wisdom Shapes Business, Economies, Societies and Nations*. New York, Doubleday.

Tan, P. J., A. Corsi, J. Cohen, A. Sharp, L. Lockshin, W. Caruso and S. Bogomolova (2018). Assessing the sales effectiveness of differently located endcaps in a supermarket. *Journal of Retailing and Consumer Services*, **43**: 200–208.

Tanusondjaja, A., M. Nenycz-Thiel, J. Dawes and R. Kennedy (2018a). Does size matter? How product portfolio size is related to brand penetration and revenue. Report 80 for Corporate Sponsors. Adelaide, Ehrenberg-Bass Institute for Marketing Science.

Tanusondjaja, A., M. Nenycz-Thiel, J. Dawes and R. Kennedy (2018b). Portfolios: Patterns in brand penetration, market share, and hero product variants. *Journal of Retailing and Consumer Services*, **41**: 211–217.

Tanusondjaja, A., G. Trinh and J. Romaniuk (2016). Exploring the past behaviour of new brand buyers. *International Journal of Market Research*, **58**(5): 733–748.

Tran, T. P., C. P. Furner and P. A. Albinsson (2020). Understanding drivers and outcomes of brand attachment in mobile branded apps. *Journal of Consumer Marketing*.

Trembath, R., J. Romaniuk and L. Lockshin (2011). Building the destination brand: An empirical comparison of two approaches. *Journal of Travel and Tourism Marketing*, **28**(8): 804–816.

Trinh, G., J. Dawes and L. Lockshin (2009). Do product variants appeal to different segments of buyers within a category? *Journal of Product & Brand Management*, **18**(2): 95–105.

Trinh, G., J. Romaniuk and A. Tanusondjaja (2016). Benchmarking buyer behavior towards new brands. *Marketing Letters*, **27**(4): 743–752.

Twedt, D. (1967). How does brand awareness-attitude affect marketing strategy? *Journal of Marketing*, **31**: 64–66.

Uncles, M., R. East and W. Lomax (2010). Market share is correlated with word-of-mouth volume. *Australasian Marketing Journal*, **18**(3): 145–150.

Uncles, M., R. Kennedy, M. Nenycz-Thiel, J. Singh and S. Kwok (2012). In 25 years, across 50 categories, user profiles for directly competing brands seldom differ: Affirming Andrew Ehrenberg's principles. *Journal of Advertising Research*, **52**(2): 252–261.

Vaughan, K., V. Beal, A. M. Corsi and B. Sharp (2020). Measuring advertising's effect on mental availability. *International Journal of Market Research*: 1–17.

Vaughan, K., V. Beal and J. Romaniuk (2016). Can brand users really remember advertising more than nonusers? Testing an empirical generalization across six advertising awareness measures. *Journal of Advertising Research*, **56**(3): 311–320.

Victory, K., M. Nenycz-Thiel, J. Dawes, A. Tanusondjaja and A. M. Corsi (2021). How common is new product failure and when does it vary? *Marketing Letters*, **32**(1): 17–32.

Wight, S. T. (2010). Brand awareness metrics: The underlying awareness of brand users and non-users. Master of Business (Research, Marketing), University of South Australia.

Wilson, A. L., C. Nguyen, S. Bogomolova, B. Sharp and T. Olds (2019). Analysing how physical activity competes: A cross-disciplinary application of the duplication of behaviour law. *International Journal of Behavioral Nutrition and Physical Activity*, **16**(1): 1–13.

Winchester, M. and J. Romaniuk (2003). Evaluative and descriptive response patterns to negative image attributes. *International Journal of Market Research*, **45**(1): 21–34.

Winchester, M. and J. Romaniuk (2008). Negative brand beliefs and brand usage. *International Journal of Market Research*, **50**(3): 355–375.

Winchester, M., J. Romaniuk and S. Bogomolova (2008). Positive and negative brand beliefs and brand defection/uptake. *European Journal of Marketing*, **42**(5/6): 553–570.

Wright, M. and B. Klÿn (1998). Environmental attitude: Behaviour correlations in 21 countries. *Journal of Empirical Generalisations in Marketing Science*, **3**(3): 42–60.

Wright, M. and M. MacRae (2007). Bias and variability in purchase intention scales. *Journal of the Academy of Marketing Science*, **35**(4): 617–624.

Yoo, B. and N. Donthu (2001). Developing and validating a multidimensional consumer-based brand equity scale. *Journal of Business Research*, **52**(1): 1–14.

Zajonc, R. B. (1968). Attitudinal effects of mere exposure. *Journal of Personality and Social Psychology*, **9**(2): 1.